Uncovering
the Original Text
of the Book of Mormon

History and Findings
of the Critical Text Project

EDITED BY

M. Gerald Bradford
and Alison V. P. Coutts

THE FOUNDATION FOR ANCIENT RESEARCH AND MORMON STUDIES

BRIGHAM YOUNG UNIVERSITY

PROVO, UTAH

2002

Photographs used by permission:

The Book of Mormon Critical Text Project
The Community of Christ
The Wilford Wood Foundation
The Harold B. Lee Library

LIBRARY OF CONGRESS CATALOGUING-IN-PUBLICATION DATA

Uncovering the original text of the Book of Mormon : history and findings of the critical text project / edited by M. Gerald Bradford and Alison V. P. Coutts.
  p. cm.
Includes bibiliographical references.
ISBN 0−934893−68−3 (alk. paper)
  1. Book of Mormon—Criticism, Textual. I. Bradford, Miles Gerald.
II. Coutts, Alison V. P.

BX8627.U53 2002
289.3′22—dc21

2002008406

PRINTED IN THE UNITED STATES OF AMERICA

FIRST EDITION

Table of Contents

Contributors

ROYAL SKOUSEN is Professor of Linguistics and English Language at Brigham Young University. In 1972 he received his Ph.D. in linguistics from the University of Illinois at Champaign-Urbana. He has published three books on linguistic theory, including *Analogical Modeling of Language* (1989) and *Analogy and Structure* (1992). He has also taught at the University of Illinois, the University of Texas, the University of California at San Diego, and the University of Tampere in Finland as a Fulbright lecturer. In 2001 he was a research fellow at the Max Planck Institute in the Netherlands, working on quantum computing and analogical modeling. Since 1988 Skousen has been the editor of the Book of Mormon critical text project.

ROBERT J. ESPINOSA was educated at Washington University, St. Louis, and at the University of New Mexico, with a B.A. in Latin American Studies. He studied hand bookbinding at the Center for Book Arts, New York City, before joining the Conservation Department of the Library of Congress, where he worked as a senior rare books conservator (1978–82). He was Head of Conservation at the Harold B. Lee Library, Brigham Young University, 1982–98, and currently is the Digital Projects Librarian for the L. Tom Perry Special Collections in the Harold B. Lee Library. From 1986 to 1998, Espinosa edited *The Book and Paper Group Annual* for the American Institute for Conservation. He has published widely on the conservation of rare books.

RONALD E. ROMIG is Archivist for the Community of Christ (formerly the Reorganized Church of Jesus Christ of Latter Day Saints), headquartered in Independence, Missouri. He administers the church's official records and papers in addition to its significant historical documentary collection. He has served as the president of the John Whitmer Historical Association and has been a council member of the Mormon History Association. He is currently vice-president of the Missouri Mormon Frontier Foundation. Romig received his M.A. from the University of Akron as well as archival training through Drake University. He is the author of a number of scholarly articles on the history of the Restoration movement.

LARRY W. DRAPER is Curator of Americana and Mormonism in the L. Tom Perry Special Collections in the Harold B. Lee Library at Brigham Young University. In 1976 he received a B.A. in philosophy from California State University at Fresno. Two years later he received a Masters of Library Science from BYU, followed in 1988 by an M.A. in history, also from BYU. For 18 years Draper worked in the LDS Church Historical Department, first as a manuscript cataloger, then from 1984 to 1997 as rare book librarian. He has held his present position at BYU since 1997.

DANIEL C. PETERSON is Associate Professor of Arabic and Islamic Studies at Brigham Young University. He is the editor-in-chief of BYU's Middle Eastern Texts Initiative, which includes the Islamic Translation Series. He earned his Ph.D. in Near Eastern Languages and Cultures from the University of California at Los Angeles. He is also the author of several books and numerous articles on Islamic and Latter-day Saint topics. Peterson currently serves on the board of the Institute for the Study and Preservation of Ancient Religious Texts and recently completed a lengthy term as chairman of the board of trustees for FARMS. He is well known as the editor of the *FARMS Review of Books.*

Introduction

WHEN THE history of Book of Mormon scholarship is written, it is certain that 2001 will be singled out for special attention since in the spring of that year the first two volumes in Royal Skousen's ambitious Book of Mormon critical text project were published.[1] After thirteen years of careful research and writing and with the help of several of his colleagues and the cooperation of a number of organizations—in particular, the Church of Jesus Christ of Latter-day Saints, Brigham Young University, and the Community of Christ (formerly the Reorganized Church of Jesus Christ of Latter Day Saints)—Skousen, a respected linguist and professor at BYU,[2] published a detailed, analytical transcription of the original manuscript *(The Original Manuscript of the Book of Mormon: Typographical Facsimile of the Extant Text)* and the printer's manuscript *(The Printer's Manuscript of the Book of Mormon: Typographical Facsimile of the Entire Text in Two Parts).*

Within the next few years, two additional companion volumes will appear: *The History of the Text of the Book of Mormon,* which will deal with the transmission of the text through all of its major editions; and an *Analysis of Textual Variants of the Book of Mormon,* along with an electronic collation that will include a lined-up comparison of important textual sources and that will specify every textual variant found in the two manuscripts and in twenty subsequent major editions. This collective endeavor is unparalleled in Book of Mormon scholarship. It will make available to researchers, scholars, teachers, and students the earliest primary sources needed for ongoing study of this foundational Latter-day Saint scripture.

In October 2001, the Foundation for Ancient Research and Mormon Studies (FARMS), along with a number of other units on the BYU campus,[3] sponsored a symposium in celebration of this publication event. Entitled "The Original Text of the Book of Mormon: Findings from the Critical Text Project," the event was well attended, reflecting widespread interest in the project. Skousen, in the first of two presentations, reviewed the history of the project and outlined his major findings and conclusions as well as his plans for future volumes. In his second presentation, he spelled out how systematic the original text of the Book of Mormon is.

The symposium also provided an occasion to hear reports from three colleagues who worked closely with Skousen on the project: Robert Espinosa, Digital Projects Librarian in Special Collections at Brigham Young University's Harold B. Lee Library; Ron Romig, Archivist for the Community of Christ in Independence, Missouri; and Larry Draper, Curator of Americana and Mormonism in Special Collections at the Harold B. Lee Library.

The program concluded with reflections on the implications of this work by two recognized Book of Mormon scholars: Richard L. Anderson, Emeritus Professor of Ancient Scripture, BYU; and Daniel C. Peterson, Associate Professor of Arabic and Islamic Studies, BYU, and editor of the *FARMS Review of Books*.

In order to make these important and insightful presentations available to an even wider audience, we have decided to publish this special report. It contains edited versions of most of what was presented at the symposium.

In the first paper, "History of the Critical Text Project of the Book of Mormon," Skousen specifies briefly what "critical textual studies" entail and how he employed this approach in his study of the English-language text of the Book of Mormon. He points out that the objective of the project is twofold: first, to determine the original English-language text (as reflected in the original manuscript, the printer's manuscript, and the early editions of the Book of Mormon), and second, to establish a history of the text that will identify accidental errors as well as editorial changes the text has undergone from the manuscripts through its various editions, from 1830 to the present.

Skousen traces the key events in the history of the work he and his colleagues have done on the Book of Mormon critical text project—from the challenges facing them in gaining access to the manuscripts and analyzing the significant number of textual variants that were discovered, to researching, writing, and carefully preparing and publishing the transcriptions of the original manuscript and the printer's manuscript.

Skousen concludes by summarizing some of the important findings that have emerged from his study. He observes that the original text shows examples of Hebraistic literalisms that are completely uncharacteristic of English; that the 1830 edition of the Book of Mormon was directly used to revise the text of the book of Isaiah in the Joseph Smith Translation of the Bible; and that included in the loss of the 116 pages of the original manuscript was not only the book of Lehi, but also most of the first two original chapters of the book of Mosiah. He contends that while some conjectures about how the original text may have read are probably correct, the original text cannot be fully recovered by human means, and that even if we had the entire original manuscript, there would still be some errors in the text mainly because the original manuscript itself contains some errors.

The next three selections ("Fragments of the Original Manuscript," by Robert Espinosa; "The Printer's Manuscript," by Ron Romig; and "Book of Mormon Editions," by Larry Draper) recount the role these authors played in collaborating with Skousen, particularly in the early stages of this project. Collectively they give the reader an insider view into the kind and range of meticulous, detailed work that was done on the manuscripts themselves, the corresponding efforts undertaken to ensure the long-term preservation of these priceless documents, and the careful review and analysis made not only of the publication of the 1830 edition but also of subsequent published editions of the Book of Mormon, all of which was needed to enable Skousen to bring the project to this point.

Based on his carefully prepared transcriptions of the original and printer's manuscripts and on his study of the first and subsequent published editions of the Book of Mormon, Skousen has proposed a number of informed and carefully reasoned textual changes. This is the subject of his second paper, "The Systematic Text of the Book of Mormon." He points out that while such proposed changes do not affect the message or doctrine of the Book of Mormon, many of them are grounded in what he has come to appreciate as the significant internal consistency of the original English-language text of the Book of Mormon.

Illustrating his observations with numerous examples, Skousen emphasizes that many of his proposed changes are based on such factors as semantically preferred readings found in the manuscripts, on instances where phraseology found in the original text is strongly supported by all other usage or where phraseology in the original text was perfectly consistent but has been altered over time due to printing errors or editing changes that have crept into subsequent editions, and on the need to further improve on punctuation—a feature not included in the original manuscript. In his paper, Skousen also deals with several what he terms "conjectural emendations"—proposed improvements in the text for which there is no direct evidence in the manuscripts or early editions. He devises rather strict, conservative criteria on the basis of which such changes need to be assessed and argues for acceptance of a number of them. Skousen concludes by repeating one of the important points he made in his earlier paper, namely, because we only have approximately 28 percent of the original manuscript, and because textual errors generally cannot be found except in reference to correct readings in the earliest textual sources, "the original English-language text of the Book of Mormon is not fully recoverable by human effort." He also points out that while conjecture, based on internal analysis of the Book of Mormon text, has proven to be largely unsuccessful in recovering the correct reading, nevertheless, some carefully reasoned conjectures are probably correct. According to Skousen, the systematic nature of the original text of the Book of Mormon supports the claim that the scripture was revealed to Joseph Smith word for word. And while there is clear evidence of some errors in the original manuscript, most mistakes can be traced to subsequent transmissions of the text, all of which have been subject to human error. The important point, however, is that none of these errors significantly interfere with the teachings of the book, nor have they "prevented readers of the book from receiving their own personal witness of its truth."

Finally, the concluding paper in this special report focuses on one of the most significant findings to emerge from the Book of Mormon critical text project, namely, that a careful study of the original and printer's manuscripts supports traditional accounts of how the Book of Mormon came about. Daniel C. Peterson, in "What the Manuscripts and the Eyewitnesses Tell Us about the Translation of the Book of Mormon," builds on Skousen's work[4] to show that the evidence of the manuscripts themselves supports the long-held claim that the text of the scripture was revealed to Joseph Smith word for word, that he relied on the use of interpreting devices in the process, and that what he saw (possibly as many as twenty to thirty words at a time) was read off by him to his scribes. At the same time, this documentary evidence provides no support for alternative explanations that Joseph Smith composed the text himself or that he took it from some other existing manuscript.

As one Latter-day Saint writer recently put it, quoting Joseph Smith, " 'Take away the Book of Mormon and the revelations and where is our religion? We have none.' And why must *that* be so? It's because the revealed witness of Jesus Christ, which the Holy Ghost confirms to anyone who has personal knowledge of the Book of Mormon and faith unto repentance, is the key to everything of worth in our religion. Without that witness, needless to say, the Book of Mormon is nothing but paper and ink; it's only black marks on a white background unless the Spirit of the Lord brings it to life in the hearts and minds of its readers."[5]

For a number of years now, Skousen and his colleagues have been, if you will, intensely dealing with the Book of Mormon as "black marks on a white background." And look at what they have accomplished! We now have a definitive transcription of all that is extant of the manuscripts of the Book of Mormon; we have a solid linguistic, documentary foundation upon which to conduct further studies of this sacred scripture; and as a result of studies produced so far, we have, as Skousen testifies, "important evidence that the Book of Mormon is a revealed text from the Lord." Such scholarship on the Book of Mormon can never claim to do more than add to our understanding of, and deepen our appreciation for, what the Lord has revealed. But for this we can be thankful indeed.

Several people helped produce this special report. The authors themselves worked tirelessly with us to ensure the details are presented as accurately as possible. The illustrations were created by Michael Lyon with graphic enhancements by Andrew Livingston and Nathan Allison in consultation with Louis Crandall. Indeed we are indebted to the Crandall Historical Printing Museum in Provo, Utah, and for Louis's painstaking efforts to help us understand the physical details of printing the Book of Mormon. Louis and his museum are an invaluable resource, and we are grateful for his willingness to share his findings with us.

—THE EDITORS
July 2002

NOTES

1. The first two volumes in this series were published by the Foundation for Ancient Research and Mormon Studies (FARMS). The Foundation will also publish the subsequent volumes. To a growing list of significant work on the Book of Mormon published by FARMS since its founding in 1979 can now been added these volumes in the Book of Mormon critical text project. Those interested in the history of Book of Mormon scholarship should read Noel B. Reynolds, "The Coming Forth of the Book of Mormon in the Twentieth Century," *BYU Studies* 38/2 (1999): 6–47.

2. Royal Skousen is uniquely qualified to undertake such an ambitious, detailed study of the text of the Book of Mormon. A professor of linguistics and English language at BYU (since 1979), Skousen took his Ph.D. from the University of Illinois, Champaign-Urbana, in 1972. Skousen is internationally recognized for his work in linguistics and related studies, having published three major books on the subject. During the spring of 2001 he was a research fellow at the Max Planck Institute in Nijmegen, the Netherlands, doing research in quantum computing and analogical modeling of language.

3. In addition to FARMS, the following organizations sponsored this symposium: the Harold B. Lee Library, the College of Humanities, the English Department, the Linguistics Department, the Religious Studies Center, and the Joseph Fielding Smith Institute for LDS History.

4. See Royal Skousen, "Translating the Book of Mormon: Evidence from the Original Manuscript," in *Book of Mormon Authorship Revisited: The Evidence for Ancient Origins,* ed. Noel B. Reynolds (Provo, Utah: FARMS, 1997), 61–93; and "How Joseph Smith Translated the Book of Mormon: Evidence from the Original Manuscript," in *Journal of Book of Mormon Studies* 7/1 (1998): 22–31.

5. H. Curtis Wright, *Things of Redeeming Worth* (Provo, Utah: BYU Religious Studies Center, 2002), 66.

History of the Critical Text Project of the Book of Mormon

ROYAL SKOUSEN

A Critical Text for the Book of Mormon

Critical texts have previously been prepared for important historical and literary works, but until fairly recently, not for the Book of Mormon. The first critical text of the Book of Mormon was published by the Foundation for Ancient Research and Mormon Studies (or FARMS) in 1984–86. That first version, although preliminary, helped to establish criteria for the current project, especially the need for direct access to the original and printer's manuscripts as well as the clearest photographs of those manuscripts.

A critical text shows all the substantive changes that a written work has undergone, from its original version to its present editions. The word *critical* is derived from the Greek word *kritḗs,* meaning "judge." When referring to a critical text, the term means that notes accompany the text so that the reader can see how the work has changed over time and thus judge between alternative readings.

There are two main goals for a critical text of the Book of Mormon. The first is to determine, to the extent possible, the original English-language text of the book. The second purpose is to establish the history of the text, including both accidental errors and editorial changes that the book has undergone as it has been transmitted down through time in its many editions.

I use the term *original text* to refer to the English-language text that Joseph Smith received by means of the interpreters and the seer stone. The term will not be used to refer to the actual ancient language that Mormon, Moroni, Nephi, and others wrote on the plates. We have no direct record of their ancient language, but we should also recognize that we actually have no direct record of the original English-language translation either. The closest source for what Joseph received is the original manuscript of the Book of Mormon, the manuscript that the scribes wrote down as Joseph dictated the English-language text. But we must not assume that the original manuscript is identical to what Joseph Smith received. Joseph had to read off the text, and the scribe had to understand his words and then write them down correctly. As we shall see, even the original manuscript contains errors in transmission.

Fragments of the original manuscript of the Book of Mormon (Helaman 15:9–14), with penciled-in punctuation added by John Gilbert, the typesetter for the 1830 edition. From Helaman 13 through Mormon 9, the 1830 edition was set from the original manuscript, not the printer's manuscript. Photograph by David Hawkinson; fragments owned by the Wilford Wood family.

But a more serious difficulty is that most of the original manuscript no longer exists. Of course, the first 116 pages of manuscript were originally lost by Martin Harris during the early summer of 1828. But the Lord prepared for this loss by having Nephi and his successors record a different version of their early history on a second set of plates (the small plates of Nephi). During the spring and early summer of 1829, Joseph Smith finished the translation, including that of the small plates.

In 1841 Joseph Smith placed the original manuscript in the cornerstone of the Nauvoo House. When removed by Lewis Bidamon in 1882, the manuscript had largely been destroyed by mold and water seepage. Today only 28 percent of the original manuscript is extant. Most of the surviving leaves and fragments (25 of the 28 percent) are held by the Church of Jesus Christ of Latter-day Saints (referred to hereafter in this article as the church). The remaining 3 percent are fragments owned by the Wilford Wood Foundation, the University of Utah, and various individuals.

Joseph Smith directed his scribes to produce a copy of the original manuscript from which the 1830 edition would be typeset. This copy is referred to as the printer's manuscript and was produced from August 1829 to the early part of 1830. For the most part, the printer set the type for the 1830 edition from the printer's manuscript, although for one sixth of the text (from Helaman 13 through the end of Mormon), the type was set from the original manuscript. The printer's manuscript is virtually 100 percent extant and is held by the Reorganized Church of Jesus Christ of Latter Day Saints (recently renamed the Community of Christ).

Errors entered the text in copying the printer's manuscript from the original manuscript. Oliver Cowdery and other scribes made an average of two to three textual changes per manuscript page. The term *textual change* means an alteration in the wording (however minor) or a consistent change in the spelling of a name. The 1830 printer also made various errors in copying the text from the manuscripts. In general, these early transmission errors have not been caught by later editors of the text except by reference to the manuscripts themselves.

We therefore have the following early stages in transmitting the Book of Mormon text:

- Joseph Smith sees the text
- Joseph reads off the text
- the scribe hears Joseph's words
- the scribe writes down the words (the original manuscript)

- the scribe copies the text (the printer's manuscript)
- the 1830 printer sets the type from manuscript, as follows:

  from the printer's manuscript, for five-sixths of the text:

    1 Nephi 1 – Helaman 13

    Ether 1 – Moroni 10

  from the original manuscript, for one-sixth of the text:

    Helaman 13 – Mormon 9

There is also evidence that for several of these stages the copying process was proofed:

- the scribe read back to Joseph Smith what had just been written down in the original manuscript
- after copying, the printer's manuscript was frequently proofed against the original manuscript (sometimes by a different scribe)
- the 1830 printed sheets were proofed against the manuscript used to set the type, although in one case the sheet was set from the printer's manuscript but then checked against the original manuscript (gathering 22, covering Alma 41–46)

Despite these efforts to assure accuracy, errors still occurred.

Our sources for recovering the original English-language text are the two manuscripts and the first three editions:

1. the original manuscript (28 percent extant)

   largely intact sheets:

     1 Nephi 2–13

     1 Nephi 15 – 2 Nephi 1

     Alma 22–60

     Alma 62 – Helaman 3

   fragments:

     1 Nephi 14

     2 Nephi 4–5

     2 Nephi 5–9, 23–25, 33

     Jacob, Enos

     Alma 10–13, 19–20

     Alma 19

     Alma 58–60

     Alma 61–62

     Helaman 13 – 3 Nephi 4

     3 Nephi 19–21, 26–27

     Ether 3–15

2. the printer's manuscript (virtually 100 percent extant)

   includes Joseph Smith's own handwritten editing for the 1837 edition

3. 1830 edition, especially for Helaman 13 – Mormon 9

4. 1837 edition, involving Joseph Smith's editing of the text into more standard English

5. 1840 edition, involving some additional editing by Joseph Smith
    includes the restoration of several phrases that had been accidentally deleted in copying from the original manuscript to the printer's manuscript

All other editions are secondary in recovering the original text. Nonetheless, these other editions are important for establishing the history and subsequent development of the text, especially its editing.

Important Events in the History of the Project

I. The first critical text of the Book of Mormon appears

1984–1986	Under the editorship of Robert (Bob) Smith, FARMS produced the first critical text. This critical text was preliminary in many respects. First of all, only microfilmed versions of the manuscripts were available; in the case of the original manuscript, the microfilm was largely unreadable; in other words, there was no access to clear photographs of the original manuscript, nor was there any access to the manuscripts themselves. Secondly, variants in the text were discovered by visually comparing the editions; there was no computerized comparison of editions.
March 1988	At the Deseret Language and Linguistic Society annual meeting in 1988, a symposium on the FARMS critical text was organized. Participants were John (Jack) Welch, Lyle Fletcher, and myself. In my presentation, I proposed to do a second critical text, one that would rely on clear photographs of the manuscripts and a computerized collation of the manuscripts and editions.

II. Getting access to the basic textual sources

17 May 1988	I met with Jack Welch, John Sorenson, and Noel Reynolds—the executive committee of FARMS at that time—and they agreed to support me in doing a second critical text. Jack agreed to see about arranging with the church to get the best possible photographs for studying the original manuscript.
20 May 1988	Three days later, I received on loan from the church's Historical Department a set of black-and-white ultraviolet photographs of the original manuscript. Most of these photographs had been taken around 1950. During the summer I began using the photos to make a transcript of the original manuscript. At the same time, an independent transcript for the manuscript was made, first by Lyle Fletcher and later by Marcello Hunter.
summer 1988	During that same summer I began selecting the editions of the Book of Mormon for which electronic versions would be produced. Larry Draper, then the rare book librarian at the Historical Department, played an instrumental role in gaining access to most of the editions. Under the direction of Mel Smith, about 15 editions were scanned at the Humanities Research Center at BYU. One was electronically keyed in. The rest

were early 1900 editions that were visually examined for differences. In all, 21 editions have been put into electronic format. Fourteen are LDS editions (from the first edition in 1830 to the current LDS edition, dating from 1981). Six are RLDS editions (from the first RLDS edition in 1874 to a modern-English edition published in 1966). And finally, there is the privately published Wright edition, printed in 1858 in New York City. All these electronic versions have been proofed at least twice.

October 1988

In the fall of 1988, Jack Welch also arranged for the RLDS Archives to loan the project a large photographic reproduction of the printer's manuscript. An independent transcript of this manuscript was made by Lawrence Skousen.

The transcripts of both the original and printer's manuscripts were keyed in directly from the photos themselves. I specifically decided that the transcripts would never be produced by correcting an already keyed-in electronic version of some other early text, such as the 1830 edition or the printer's manuscript (both of which existed at the time). Later, the two transcripts of each manuscript were checked against

The enlarged photocopy of the printer's manuscript. The photo also shows an original copy of the 1830 edition.

each other and differences reconciled. Since then, the transcripts have been checked several times by myself, Matt Empey, Christina Skousen, and Lawrence Skousen.

III. Getting access to the actual manuscripts, including newly discovered fragments

April 1991

In the fall of 1990, after completing the initial transcript for the printer's manuscript, I realized that I needed to examine the actual document and compare my transcript with the printer's manuscript itself. Ron Romig, archivist for the Community of

Royal Skousen, the editor of the Book of Mormon critical text project, comparing his transcript against the actual printer's manuscript of the Book of Mormon, April 1991, Independence, Missouri. Photograph by Ron Romig.

Christ, prepared the way by arranging for the manuscript to be brought from the Kansas City bank vault that it was being stored in. Our visit to Independence, Missouri, was scheduled for April 1991. Ron and my wife Sirkku did the physical examination of the manuscript, while I checked the transcript. Seeing the actual manuscript made a huge difference. Photographs do not always tell the truth, especially black and white ones. Originally, we had planned a week-long visit, but I soon realized that the work would take longer, so we ended up spending two weeks in Independence. Even that was barely adequate.

summer 1991   Later that summer, I made several visits to the Wilford Wood Museum in Bountiful, Utah. Bob Smith, in the first critical edition, had noted that the museum had some "unknown very small fragments" of the original manuscript. After examining the fragments—a clump of unreadable pieces of paper wrapped in cellophane—I enlisted the help of Robert Espinosa (then head of conservation at the Harold B. Lee Library) and David Hawkinson (then the photographer for the Museum of Art), and we arranged with the Wilford Wood family to conserve and photograph the fragments at the Harold B. Lee Library.

fall 1991   On 30 September 1991, we began a three-week period of intense work on the fragments in the Harold B. Lee Library. Robert Espinosa, with the help of his assistants, separated the fragments. After being humidified, unfolded, and flattened, the fragments were photographed by David Hawkinson. Black-and-white ultraviolet photography proved the most successful in bringing out the faded ink on the fragments. Robert also identified the paper type for each fragment, except for the very smallest ones. Finally, the fragments were encapsulated in Mylar and returned to the Wilford Wood family. These fragments are from six different places in the original manuscript. They come from 29 leaves (or 58 pages) of the manuscript and account for two percent of the text.

David Hawkinson, then photographer for the Museum of Art, Brigham Young University, preparing to photograph the Lyman Wight petition, one of the Wilford Wood fragments, using reflected ultraviolet light, October 1991. Photograph by Nevin Skousen.

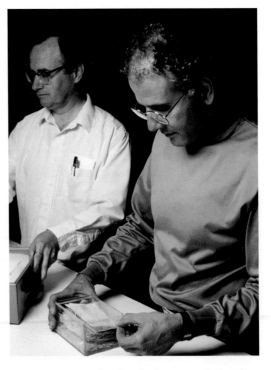

Robert Espinosa, then head of conservation at the Harold B. Lee Library, Brigham Young University, examining the box containing the Wilford Wood fragments, 30 September 1991. Royal Skousen, editor of the project, is standing by. Photograph by David Hawkinson.

Nevin Skousen, preparing to photograph one of the pages of the printer's manuscript, October 1992, Independence, Missouri. Photograph by Royal Skousen.

Ron Romig, archivist for the Community of Christ, collecting color prints of photographs of the printer's manuscript, October 1992, Orem, Utah. Photograph by Royal Skousen.

November 1991   Later that year Brent Ashworth brought in his fragment from Alma 60 to be conserved and photographed. At that time we also examined three different forgeries of fragments of the original manuscript that Brent had acquired.

October 1992   By 1992 I realized that what I needed was a set of color photographs of the printer's manuscript, so I arranged for a second visit to Independence in October 1992. My brother Nevin Skousen (a professional photographer, now deceased) photographed the entire manuscript at the RLDS Church Library. Later that month, with the assistance of Ron Romig, two sets of prints were made here in Utah, one of which was loaned to the critical text project.

June 1994   Finally, in June 1994, I arranged for a one-week visit to Independence so that Robert Espinosa could make a detailed comparison of the paper types of both manuscripts. The church and the Wilford Wood family provided samples of small fragments from the original manuscript so that an on-site comparison could be made.

November 1995   The following year, the Ada Cheney fragments of the original manuscript were conserved and photographed at the Harold B. Lee Library. These fragments come from two leaves in Alma 58–60.

1993–1996	Throughout this period, I spent considerable time hunting for additional fragments of the original manuscript, especially the Joseph Summerhays fragment, a half leaf from 1 Nephi 14–15. I also made a visit to Florida to check out the provenance of the Ruth Smith fragment (from 2 Nephi 4–5), now held by the church. And more time was spent identifying forgeries of fragments purporting to be from the original manuscript. One striking contrast was observed when the University of Chicago acquisition was examined and compared with the Wilford Wood fragments—namely, the two leaves supposedly from Alma 3–5 showed several dozen unique properties, ones that I had not seen anywhere else in either of the two Book of Mormon manuscripts, whereas the legitimate Wilford Wood fragments from 58 pages of the original manuscript showed only one unique property.
1993–1997	Also during this period, from 1993 to 1997, I compared the initial transcript of the original manuscript against the actual intact sheets of the original manuscript, as well as many fragments, at the Historical Department in Salt Lake City. There were also numerous attempts to rephotograph some parts of the manuscript, but this proved largely unsuccessful. Later, with the help of Gene Ware of the College of Engineering and Technology at BYU, selected parts of the original manuscript were examined using multispectral imaging.
1998	Later, in 1998, Gene was also able to do multispectral imaging for selected parts of the printer's manuscript. This additional examination of the printer's manuscript occurred at the Historical Department, while the manuscript was being conserved for the Community of Christ.

IV. Analyzing the textual variants

From August 1995 through March 1999, I prepared a computerized collation for the entire text of the Book of Mormon. This lined-up comparison lists every variant for the two manuscripts and twenty editions of the Book of Mormon, from the 1830 edition to the current LDS and Community of Christ (RLDS) editions of the book. Not only are textual changes noted, but also every change in punctuation, spelling, capitalization, and versification. During this same period of time, I prepared a preliminary analysis of the changes in the text. This document, 3650 pages long, discusses the evidence for about 1500 proposed changes in the current text.

The large majority of these textual changes involve minor variation in phraseology. For instance, in more than a few cases, the indefinite article *a* has accidentally been omitted, especially when the article is repeated in a coordinate construction. In the following list, we have eight examples involving a pair of coordinated adjectives followed by a noun. For each case, the edition in which the repeated *a* was first dropped is listed in parentheses:

Omni 1:28	a strong and **a** mighty man > a strong and mighty man (1852)
Mosiah 27:7	a large and **a** wealthy people > a large and wealthy people (1840)

Alma 11:26	a true and **a** living God >
	a true and living God (1837)
Alma 11:27	a true and **a** living God >
	a true and living God (1841)
Alma 12:22	a lost and **a** fallen people >
	a lost and fallen people (1852)
Alma 43:6	a more wicked and **a** murderous disposition >
	a more wicked and murderous disposition (1841)
Mormon 9:4	a holy and **a** just God >
	a holy and just God (1830)
Ether 1:34	a large and **a** mighty man >
	a large and mighty man (1852)

In contrast to cases of minor variation, about 100 newly discovered changes are semantically significant. These proposed changes lead to differences in meaning, ones that would show up when translating the text.

V. Information to the Church Scriptures Committee

1994	In 1994, the church requested that I, as editor of the critical text project, take a full-time leave from my teaching responsibilities at BYU and work full time on this project. Such a leave would allow me to get the project done sooner and would also allow me to share my findings with the Church Scriptures Committee.
February 1995	In February 1995 I signed an agreement with the church and BYU that, as editor of the project, I would convey information to the Church Scriptures Committee about possible changes to the text. The agreement specifically provided that the church and BYU would guarantee the independence of the project—as editor, I would (1) hold the copyright to the critical text and (2) exercise complete control over the content of the critical text.
1995–1999	Over the next four years, as the analysis of the textual variants was written, I conveyed this information to the Church Scriptures Committee.
December 1998	Late in 1998, I made a publishing agreement with FARMS, prior to FARMS becoming a part of BYU. In this agreement, I agreed to share the copyright with FARMS. Correspondingly, FARMS agreed to allow the editor full control over the content of the critical text volumes, as well as my approval of all promotional materials.
April 2001	From August 2000 through the spring of 2001, there were additional negotiations between the church, BYU, FARMS, and myself in order to resolve complications that had arisen because FARMS had become a part of BYU. In April of 2001, an amendment to the previous agreements was made, in which I acknowledged that FARMS had become a part of BYU, but that the copyright would continue to be explicitly shared between me and FARMS. Further, it was agreed that, as editor, I would continue to exercise full editorial control, including the right to approve all promotional material.

VI. Publishing the critical text project

May 2001   Finally, in May 2001, the transcripts of the two manuscripts were officially published in two volumes, one for each manuscript:

Volume 1.   *The Original Manuscript of the Book of Mormon:*
            Typographical Facsimile of the Extant Text
                    568 pages (including 41 pages of introduction and 16 pages of
                    black-and-white ultraviolet and color photographs of fragments)

Volume 2.   *The Printer's Manuscript of the Book of Mormon:*
            Typographical Facsimile of the Entire Text in Two Parts
                    1008 pages (bound in two parts, including 36 pages of introduction
                    and 8 pages of color photographs of the manuscript)

A typographical facsimile presents an exact reproduction of the text in typescript. The text is transcribed line for line and without any corrections or expansions. Original spellings and miswritings are retained. All scribal changes in the manuscripts—whether crossouts, erasures, overwriting, or insertions—are reproduced. A continuously running text for the extant portions of the original manuscript has been provided, with conjectured text placed sublinearly. Both volumes contain introductions which present a brief history of the manuscripts, the symbols used in the transcription system (plus examples of their use), and a physical description of the manuscripts.

These two volumes present the earliest textual sources for the Book of Mormon. All known fragments of the original manuscript have been identified, interpreted, and pieced together (to the extent possible). With the publication of these two volumes, all the legitimate manuscript sources for the Book of Mormon text are now accessible. Using the first three editions of the Book of Mormon, along with these transcripts, scholars now have all the available information needed for studying the text of the Book of Mormon.

This publication is intended for scholars of all faiths and persuasions: LDS, Community of Christ (RLDS), and all others interested in the text. Both LDS and RLDS versifications have been provided in the identification of manuscript pages and photographs. The critical text project is a scholarly one and has not involved any ecclesiastical approval or endorsement. The transcripts and the textual interpretations represent the editor's own scholarly work, but have involved peer review from other scholars.

Typographer Jonathan Saltzman, designer and typesetter for the critical text of the Book of Mormon.

The design and typesetting is the work of typographer Jonathan Saltzman and presents the text in an appealing form—one appropriate to the importance of the Book of Mormon.

VII. More to come

Ultimately, there will be four printed volumes and one electronic collation in the complete critical text. In addition to the two now-published volumes, there will be:

Volume 3.   *The History of the Text of the Book of Mormon*

Volume 4.   *Analysis of Textual Variants of the Book of Mormon*

Volume 5.   *A Complete Electronic Collation of the Book of Mormon*

The third volume will discuss the transmission of the text, from the manuscripts through the major editions. The fourth volume will discuss cases of textual variance and will attempt to determine the original English-language reading of the text. The electronic collation will be a lined-up comparison of the important textual sources and will specify every textual variant in the Book of Mormon. The collation will include the readings of the two manuscripts and twenty editions of the Book of Mormon.

The editor's plan is to have volumes 3 and 4 and the electronic collation available within the next three years.

Important Findings

Now let us consider more of the important findings of this project:

(1) Scribal corrections in the original manuscript support statements made by witnesses of the translation that Joseph Smith sometimes spelled out the unfamiliar Book of Mormon names, at least on their first occurrence. For instance, when the name *Coriantumr* first appears in the book of Helaman, Oliver Cowdery first spelled it phonetically, as *Coriantummer,* then he immediately crossed out the whole name and correctly spelled it, as *Coriantumr.* This name could not have been spelled correctly unless Joseph Smith spelled it out letter by letter (or wrote it out for Oliver). In fact, Oliver ended the final *r* of the correct spelling with a huge flourish of his quill, almost as if to say "How could anybody be expected to spell such a name?"

(2) The original text is more consistent in phraseology and word usage. Many errors have led to various "wrinkles" in the text. One example is the phrase "the word of the justice of the eternal God" (in 1 Nephi 12:18), which in the original manuscript read "the sword of the justice of the eternal God":

> 1 Nephi 12:18
>
> *original manuscript*
>   & a great & a terable gulph divideth them
>   yea even the **sword** of the Justice of the Eternal God
>
> *printer's manuscript*
>   & a great & a terrible gulf divideth them
>   yea even the **word** of the Justice of the Eternal God

Elsewhere the text refers only to "the sword of God's justice," never to "the word of God's justice":

Alma 26:19	the sword of his justice
Alma 60:29	the sword of justice
Helaman 13:5	the sword of justice
Helaman 13:5	the sword of justice
3 Nephi 20:20	the sword of my justice
3 Nephi 29:4	the sword of his justice
Ether 8:23	the sword of the justice of the eternal God

Note, in particular, the last example (in Ether 8:23), which has the exact same phraseology as the example in 1 Nephi 12:18.

(3) Sometimes passages of text are the same, word for word, even though they are found in completely different parts of the book. Jack Welch has provided the following example:

1 Nephi 1:8
    and being thus overcome with the spirit
    he was carried away in a vision
    even that he saw the heavens open
    and he thought he saw
    God sitting upon his throne
    surrounded with numberless concourses of angels
    in the attitude of singing and praising their God

Alma 36:22
    yea and methought I saw
    even as our father Lehi saw
    God sitting upon his throne
    surrounded with numberless concourses of angels
    in the attitude of singing and praising their God

Both passages refer to Lehi's first vision and use precisely the same words to describe it.

(4) The original text is not fully recoverable by human effort. Textual errors are generally not found except by discovering the correct reading in the manuscripts. Unfortunately, most of the original manuscript is not extant. Conjecture based on internal analysis of the Book of Mormon text has largely been unsuccessful in recovering the correct reading. Still, some conjectures are probably correct, such as "neither happiness nor misery" in 2 Nephi 2:11 rather than the current reading ("neither holiness nor misery"):

    for it must needs be that there is an opposition in all things
    if not so—my first born in the wilderness—
    righteousness could not be brought to pass neither wickedness
    neither **holiness** nor **misery**
    neither good nor bad

Elsewhere, the text always contrasts *misery* with *happiness,* not *holiness:*

2 Nephi 2:11	*happiness* nor *misery*
2 Nephi 2:13	no righteousness nor *happiness* . . . no punishment nor *misery*
Alma 3:26	eternal *happiness* or eternal *misery*
Alma 40:15	this state of *happiness* and this state of *misery*
Alma 40:15	to *happiness* or *misery*
Alma 40:17	to *happiness* or *misery*
Alma 40:21	in *happiness* or in *misery*
Alma 41:4	raised to endless *happiness* . . . or to endless *misery*

We do not have the original manuscript in 2 Nephi 2:11. Orthographically, *holiness* and *happiness* are similar. Probably, Oliver Cowdery mistakenly read *happiness* as *holiness.* (This conjecture was first suggested by Corbin T. Volluz.)

(5) Even if we had the entire original manuscript, there could still be errors in the text, mainly because the original manuscript itself has some errors. For instance, in 1 Nephi 7:5, the original manuscript reads "Ishmael and also his hole hole," an impossible reading. The correct reading must be something else.

When copying into the printer's manuscript, Oliver Cowdery emended this phrase to "Ishmael and also his household":

1 Nephi 7:5

original manuscript
the lord did soften the hart of ishmael
and also his **hole hole**

printer's manuscript
the Lord did soften the heart of Ishmael
& also his **household**

Usage elsewhere in the text suggests the word *household* always occurs with a universal quantifier (either *all* or *whole* or none at all in negative sentences, as in the last example listed below):

1 Nephi 5:14	all his household
2 Nephi 4:10	all his household
2 Nephi 4:12	all his household
Alma 22:23	his whole household
Alma 23:3	all his household
Alma 34:21	all your household
Ether 9:3	all his household
Ether 10:1	all his household
Ether 13:20	all his household
Ether 13:21	all his household
Ether 13:22	Coriantumr repented not / neither his household
	[that is, none of his household repented]

Note, in particular, the occurrence of "his whole household" in Alma 22:23. This suggests that the original text for 1 Nephi 7:5 probably read "Ishmael and also his whole household," where the first *hole* in the original manuscript is a homophone for *whole* and the second *hole* stands for the *hold* of *household* (with loss of the final *d* in pronunciation).

(6) Errors in the original manuscript show that the scribe heard the text; that is, Joseph Smith orally dictated the text to the scribe:

	WRITTEN	INTENDED
1 Nephi 13:29	**&** exceeding great many	**an** exceeding great many
1 Nephi 17:48	wither even as a dried **weed**	wither even as a dried **reed**
Alma 55:8	he sayeth unto **him**	he sayeth unto **them**
Alma 57:22	did **meet** the Lamanites	did **beat** the Lamanites

On the other hand, corrected errors in the printer's manuscript show that the text was visually copied from the original manuscript:

	CORRECTION	CONTEXT
Mosiah 15:9	sanctified > satisfied	_____ the demands of justice
Mosiah 27:37	deliver > declare	they did _____ unto the people
Alma 34:10	sacrament > sacrifice	a great and last _____
Helaman 4:25	cause > cease	did _____ to preserve them

(7) The systematic nature of the original text and the spelling out of Book of Mormon names support the theory that the text was revealed to Joseph Smith, word for word and even letter for letter. On the other hand, all subsequent transmissions of the text appear to be subject to human error. At each stage, the accuracy of the transmission has depended upon the carefulness of the transmitter, whether Joseph Smith, his scribes, or later editors and typesetters. (This caveat, of course, equally applies to the critical text itself.) Although all have tried to do their best, every transmission of the text appears to have led to some mistakes. Yet none of these errors significantly interfere with either the message of the book or its doctrine. These textual errors have never prevented readers of the book from receiving their own personal witness of its truth.

(8) The editing of the text (including Joseph Smith's for the 1837 edition) should, in nearly all instances, be viewed as translating the text into a more standard variety of English. Moreover, in his editing of the text, Joseph acted as a human editor; his 1837 and 1840 revisions do not represent any kind of "final authorial intent" since Joseph Smith is not the author of the Book of Mormon. Nor is there any evidence that his editorial revisions represent inspired corrections to the text, especially since he left unchanged dozens of substantive errors that the scribes originally made when they copied from the original manuscript to the printer's manuscript.

(9) The original text of the Book of Mormon reflects the style of Early Modern English—namely, the biblical style from the 1500s. Nonetheless, this biblical style in the Book of Mormon is not identical to the style of the King James Bible except in those Book of Mormon passages which directly quote from the King James Bible (such as Isaiah and Matthew).

(10) The original text shows examples of Hebraistic literalisms that are completely uncharacteristic of English, such as the extra *and* found after the *if*-clause in Moroni 10:4 ("*if* ye shall ask with a sincere heart with real intent having faith in Christ **and** he will manifest the truth of it unto you"). A whole series of this usage involving the *if-and* construction is found, for example, in Helaman 12:13–21:

13   yea and *if* he sayeth unto the earth move **and** it is moved

14   yea *if* he sayeth unto the earth thou shalt go back that it lengthen out the day for many hours **and** it is done

16   and behold also *if* he sayeth unto the waters of the great deep be thou dried up **and** it is done

17   behold *if* he sayeth unto this mountain be thou raised up and come over and fall upon that city that it be buried up **and** behold it is done

19   and *if* the Lord shall say be thou accursed that no man shall find thee from this time henceforth and forever **and** behold no man getteth it henceforth and forever

20   and behold *if* the Lord shall say unto a man because of thine iniquities thou shalt be accursed forever **and** it shall be done

21   and *if* the Lord shall say because of thine iniquities thou shalt be cut off from my presence **and** he will cause that it shall be so

Beginning with the 1837 edition, all these examples of the extra *and* have been edited out of the text. Such examples of a Hebraistic *if-and* construction in the original text provide further evidence that Joseph Smith received the text word for word. If he had received only ideas, there would have been no reason to have added the non-English use of *and* in all these examples.

Fragment from 2 Nephi 7 of the original manuscript of the Book of Mormon, quoting from Isaiah 50.
For these biblical quotes, the original Book of Mormon text closely follows the reading of the King James Bible.
Photographs by David Hawkinson; fragment owned by the Wilford Wood family.

(11) The original text also shows examples of Joseph Smith's upstate New York English, which is characteristic of general American dialects, even to our own time. Over the years, this dialectal English has also been edited out of the text. Some students of the text have claimed that the Lord himself never would have revealed an ungrammatical text to Joseph Smith. It would be "blasphemy," according to B. H. Roberts, to think that the Lord would reveal his word in incorrect English. However, this argument presumes that if the Lord literally revealed the Book of Mormon text word for word, then the language would have to be in, say, B. H. Robert's "correct" English rather than Joseph Smith's own dialect. I would rather think that the Lord is no respecter of tongues (see Doctrine and Covenants 1:24).

(12) The errors in copying from the original to the printer's manuscript go against the supposed rules of textual transmission. The readings in the printer's manuscript tend to be more difficult and shorter than those in the original manuscript (rather than easier and longer, the presumption of traditional textual criticism).

(13) In copying the Isaiah quotations, the scribes frequently tended to misread individual words, as in these examples from 2 Nephi:

	ORIGINAL MANUSCRIPT	PRINTER'S MANUSCRIPT
7:2	I make **the** rivers a wilderness	I make **their** rivers a wilderness
7:5	hath **opened** mine ear	hath **appointed** mine ear
23:4	the **host** of the battle	the **hosts** of the battle
24:25	I will **break** the Assyrian	I will **bring** the Assyrian

In each case, the reading of the original manuscript is the same as that found in the King James text. This finding suggests that if there is only a single isolated word difference between the King James reading and the current reading in the Book of Mormon, we may very well have an example of a scribal error. In the following examples from 2 Nephi, the original manuscript is not extant, but may have read identically to the King James text:

	KING JAMES BIBLE	PRINTER'S MANUSCRIPT
23:15	every one that is **found**	every one that is **proud**
24:19	**raiment** of those that are slain	**remnant** of those that are slain

(14) The 1830 edition of the Book of Mormon was directly used to revise the text of the book of Isaiah in the Joseph Smith Translation (or JST) of the Bible, thus introducing errors into the JST that had earlier crept into the Book of Mormon text during its transmission. For instance, in 2 Nephi 7:5, the King James Bible and the original manuscript read "the Lord God hath opened mine ear," while the printer's manuscript, the 1830 edition, and the JST incorrectly read "the Lord God hath appointed mine ear(s)."

(15) Joseph Smith acted as scribe for 28 words of the original manuscript (in Alma 45:22). These words are apparently the earliest extant writing in Joseph Smith's own hand. Here Joseph seems to have temporarily taken over for Oliver Cowdery. The number of words copied by Joseph agrees with other evidence we have that Joseph Smith could see from 20 to 30 words at a time. For instance, the following example of scribal anticipation (immediately crossed out) shows that Joseph must have attempted to dictate 20 words at one time to his scribe, Oliver Cowdery:

Alma 56:41

      & it came to pass that again \<we saw the Lamanites\>
      when the light of the morning came we saw the Lamanites upon us

(16) The word *chapter* was not original to the Book of Mormon text, but was apparently added whenever Joseph Smith saw some indication of a break in the text. The chapter numbers themselves were often added months later. The break at the beginning of 2 Nephi shows that Joseph was not immediately aware that 1 Nephi had actually ended:

               \<Chapter \<{V\|I}\> VIII\>
     second   Chapter I
    The ^ Book of Nephi ^ An account of the death of Lehi . . .

Further, the specification of a chapter number for the small books of Enos, Omni, and Jarom shows that Joseph Smith was reading off the text and did not know in advance how long a book would be or how many chapters it would contain.

(17) Along with the loss of the first 116 pages of the original manuscript (which contained the book of Lehi), most of the original first two chapters of the book of Mosiah were also apparently lost. In the printer's manuscript, the beginning of Mosiah was originally designated as chapter III. In addition, the title of the book ("the Book of Mosiah") was later inserted between the lines:

             the Book of Mosiah
    peace in the land ~~~~~ Chapter I\<II\> ~~~~~ And now there was no more . . .

The loss of the first two chapters explains why the book begins in the middle of things:

Mosiah 1:1

      and now there was no more contention in all the land of Zarahemla
      among all the people which belonged to king Benjamin
      so that king Benjamin had continual peace all the remainder of his days

All other books start their account with the person for which the book is named, yet here the book of Mosiah begins with king Benjamin. The original book undoubtedly began with the account of a Mosiah—namely, king Benjamin's father, the first Mosiah. Further, this book is missing the initial book summary that typically begins all the other longer books.

Conclusion

There has also been a spiritual dimension to this work, although my own testimony of the Book of Mormon is not based on my work on the critical text project, but rather on my own personal witness that this book records events which really happened. About twenty-five years ago, as I was reading the Book of Mormon during a time of personal difficulty, I reread the account of Ammon, king Lamoni, and the queen in Alma 19, which records the moment when the servant woman Abish raises the queen from the ground:

Alma 19:29–30
> and it came to pass that she went and took the queen by the hand
> that perhaps she might raise her from the ground
> and as soon as she touched her hand
> she arose and stood upon her feet
> and cried with a loud voice saying
> O blessed Jesus who has saved me from an awful hell
> O blessed God have mercy on this people
> and when she had said this she clapped her hands
> being filled with joy
> speaking many words which were not understood

As I was reading this passage, the spirit personally witnessed to me, "This really happened." I have always cherished this moment in my life, and have been grateful to the Lord for the sure knowledge that the Book of Mormon is the word of the Lord.

Nonetheless, it has been a delight to have discovered evidence in the original manuscript to support what witnesses said about how Joseph Smith translated. In my initial work on the original manuscript of the Book of Mormon, I was always excited to discover the occasional error that had crept into the text. But over time I have become more amazed about the nature of the original text of the Book of Mormon. In particular, the original manuscript provides important evidence that the Book of Mormon is a revealed text from the Lord. Indeed, the consistency of the original language supports the argument that the text was revealed to the Prophet Joseph Smith, word for word. ∎

Robert Espinosa separating out the Wilford Wood fragments. Photograph by David Hawkinson.

Fragments of the Original Manuscript

ROBERT J. ESPINOSA

IN THE course of working with original documentary materials, one becomes aware that there is an eloquence in the language of the materials themselves. There is a text to be read in the materials as a whole, which no facsimile, no copy, no forgery, nothing else can reproduce. This is the wonder of working with original materials and learning to read what they have to say. Each aspect of their form—the qualities of the paper, the physical makeup, the writing medium, the marks and corrections, and all subsequent changes—is a testimony to their message. That is why the preservation of originals is so important, allowing future generations to discover for themselves the myriad layers of meaning present—and sometimes hidden—in the genuine artifact.

In order to convey the essence uncovered in the course of a careful study and reading of the whole artifact, a truly faithful rendition of original manuscripts or printed texts can be captured in the production of a critical text. This text includes information about as many aspects of the original as is possible, including all the descriptive information that can be discovered about the materials themselves. Thus an invaluable addition to the artifact itself is a complete record of a systematic study of the artifact in all its dimensions.

I was first approached by Royal Skousen in the summer of 1991 to participate in the critical text project of the Book of Mormon. At the time I was head of the conservation laboratory at Brigham Young University's Harold B. Lee Library. Royal and I discussed our laboratory's capabilities, our experience in conservation, our facilities, and our equipment. Royal outlined the scope and goals of the critical text project and also informed me of the existence of an unexamined clump of fragments in the Wilford Wood Museum in Bountiful, Utah, and the significance of these fragments to this project. The hope was that we might be able to provide some assistance in the recovery of these fragments, whose contents were as yet unknown. What was known was that they were alleged to be from the cornerstone of the Nauvoo House, in which the original manuscript of the Book of Mormon had been placed in 1841. Royal was aware of other possible fragments in private hands that might also require careful study, if not conservation intervention.

In the summer of 1991, we began negotiations with the Wilford Wood heirs, Richard W. Glade, Leilah Wood Glade, and her sister Mary Wood Cannon. We went to Bountiful to talk about the process of conserving the fragments, and, through the course of our discussions and negotiations about this project, it became clear that the conservation work, photography, and so forth, could not really be done at the Wilford Wood Museum. We invited Richard Glade to visit our laboratory to reassure the family that our interest was professional, objective, and scientific, and that we had the facilities, the equipment, and the expertise to work on these fragments and return them to the Wood family.

The confidence level that developed between the Wood family and the project staff was based on, I think, their judgment that indeed our interest was purely in recovering the text and in conserving the fragments, and that we had no designs on their ownership of the fragments. I think it was also clear to them that one unusual aspect about BYU's conservation department at that time was that none of us were members of the Church of Jesus Christ of Latter-day Saints and therefore we had no other motive for doing this work.

During the three weeks that we worked on the manuscript, security was very tight in the library and in the laboratory itself. Of course, rumors abounded on campus that things were happening in the library that were of great interest to the community. But the beautiful thing about those three weeks was the collaborative nature of the work on the original manuscript. We were working with Royal, of course, who was in charge of the project, and with David Hawkinson, a photographer from BYU's Museum of Art. Of course, my staff members (Pamela Barrios and Catherine Bell) and I were all intensely involved. We also recruited other members of the campus community who might be able to provide some

Cathy Bell, at the time a conservator in the Harold B. Lee Library, preparing a glycine envelope to hold a flattened fragment. Photograph by Robert Espinosa.

Pam Barrios, a conservator in the Harold B. Lee Library, unfolding a Wilford Wood fragment. Photograph by Robert Espinosa.

Discussing how the fragments will be conserved, 30 September 1991: Royal Skousen, editor of the critical text project; Richard Glade, grandson of Wilford Wood and representative of the family; and Robert Espinosa, head of conservation. Photograph by David Hawkinson.

Richard Glade and Royal Skousen looking on as Robert Espinosa examines the fragments wrapped in cellophane at the bottom of the Plexiglas box. Photograph by David Hawkinson.

Robert Espinosa extracting the clump of fragments by removing the staples from the cellophane wrapping. Photograph by David Hawkinson.

The clump of Wilford Wood fragments after the removal of the cellophane wrapping. Photograph by Robert Espinosa.

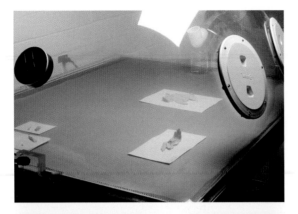

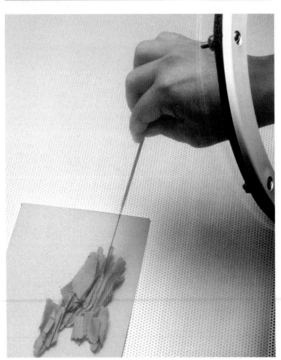

Using the ultrasonic humidifier to tease apart a large fragment from the Lyman Wight petition, also placed with the original manuscript in the cornerstone of the Nauvoo House. Photographs by Robert Espinosa.

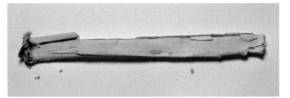

Rolled-up fragment from 2 Nephi 7–8. Photograph by Robert Espinosa.

The same fragment from 2 Nephi 7–8, now unfolded but not yet flattened. Photograph by Robert Espinosa.

The same Lyman Wight fragment (pictured left), now unfolded but not yet flattened. Photograph by David Hawkinson; fragment owned by the Wilford Wood family.

assistance or help. Leilah and Richard Glade represented the Wilford Wood family heirs. So this task brought together a team of people who really were able to work very successfully and very intensely on these fragments.

The fragments had been stored in a Plexiglas box for over fifty years, the whole time that they were in the museum at Bountiful. What we extracted from that box was a clump of fragments wrapped in cellophane. The immediate task was to figure out how to dissect this extremely fragile and brittle clump of papers and discover what might lay in these fragments. We found fragments of every size and every type of paper in this clump, which measured about 150 MM × 50MM × 15 MM.

We began by carefully separating those larger pieces that could be pried apart. The main process that we used for dissection and recovery was ultrasonic humidification. This process of moisturizing the fibers of the paper allowed the fragments to be unfolded without further damage. As the humidification process progressed, these fragments were gradually teased apart. One clump of fragments (because of its shape I humorously referred to it as the cigar fragment) contained sections from the book of Ether; it had an intact thread that had once held the whole gathering together. This gathering was very interesting and significant for Royal's work because it revealed that, for the inner side of the center sheet in the gathering, the writing of the text goes straight across both leaves. This kind of placement of the writing occurs nowhere else in either of the Book of Mormon manuscripts. Ultimately, we were able to unfold fragments from four sheets of the Ether gathering. And it is quite amazing overall that from the entire clump of papers we were able to identify fragments from fifty-eight pages of the original manuscript.

The whole laboratory was dedicated to this work during the course of the three weeks (in September and October 1991). The fragments were very carefully classified and gathered together. We noted the placement of different fragments as they came off the clump, together with any kind of association that might be helpful in terms of reconstruction. We used reflected ultraviolet photography to help read these fragments because the ink in most cases was extremely faded.

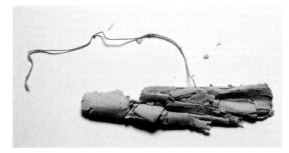

A clump of fragments from the book of Ether, still holding the original thread used to tie together a gathering of sheets. Photograph by Robert Espinosa.

Color and black-and-white ultraviolet photographs of the inner side of the center sheet from the Ether gathering (showing Ether 9–10), with the text written all the way across both leaves. Photographs by David Hawkinson; fragments owned by the Wilford Wood family.

Some of the larger fragments in the clump were not from the Book of Mormon itself but were from a petition. In other words, not every piece of paper in the clump was from the original manuscript. There were also very small fragments from an 1837 edition of the Book of Mormon as well as small fragments from a King James Bible.

One of the procedures that helped us identify and locate the fragments was examining the paper types. In the course of our work, we discovered four different paper types among the Wilford Wood fragments of the original manuscript. Actually, what we were looking for was the physical characteristics of the paper—namely, the surface texture and the wire marks, what we might call watermarking, which are the "footprints" of the production process of paper-making. These characteristics helped to distinguish one paper from the next—that is, to distinguish one paper production run from another. Paper A had a very distinct and open set of wire marks. Paper B/D had almost no distinguishable wire marks but had a very pulpy and particular formation of the fibers. Paper C had a distinct pattern of the pulp and of the wire. And paper E from the Ether gathering again had a particular kind of pulp formation.

The final step in this conservation process was to organize the fragments and to use an ultrasonic encapsulation machine to protect them in Mylar. We placed the fragments into sheets divided into four quadrants.

Having established these types of pulp and wire marks in the Wilford Wood fragments, we were later able to go to the Historical Department in Salt Lake City to make a comparison with the larger extant sheets of the original manuscript. There we found two of the same paper types (namely, A and B/D), plus one additional type of paper (labeled F) for the first part of 1 Nephi. Our analysis confirmed that each paper type was restricted to a single continuous portion of the original manuscript.

In 1994 we went to Independence, Missouri, to examine the printer's manuscript. I again carried out

The conservators working on the fragments in their lab in the Harold B. Lee Library, Brigham Young University, September–October 1991. Photograph by David Hawkinson.

Fragment from 2 Nephi 25, showing the improvement in readability when photographed in black-and-white using reflected ultraviolet light. Photographs by David Hawkinson; fragment owned by the Wilford Wood family.

Robert Espinosa checking the encapsulated fragments. Photograph by David Hawkinson.

Encapsulating some of the Wilford Wood fragments in Mylar. Photograph by Robert Espinosa.

a very careful analysis of all the physical characteristics of the paper in each gathering of that manuscript. We are fortunate in having the entire printer's manuscript. As a result we were able to verify that each gathering of the printer's manuscript always consisted of a single paper type—that is to say, no gathering was made up of two or more different paper types. There were multiple gatherings of a single paper type, but every gathering was always made from the same type of paper. Thus we were able to corroborate what we thought we had discovered in the original manuscript.

In the printer's manuscript we identified eight different types of paper. None of the paper types in the printer's manuscript seemed to correspond at all with the types of paper found in the extant portions of the original manuscript, so in all there are (at least) thirteen different types of paper in these two manuscripts.

We only have a few opportunities in our professional careers to be involved with truly significant projects that demand all our professional acumen and expertise. To work in the field of book and paper conservation affords some unique opportunities. I have worked on many great books, principally manuscripts and early printed books at the Library of Congress, one of which was the Gutenberg Bible. I have also treated the original library of Thomas Jefferson, as well as early documents of the Founding Fathers. At the Harold B. Lee Library, early Christian papyri, medieval manuscripts, and numerous early printed books have come through my hands. But no project, before or since, compares with the thrill and intensity of working on this project, whose focus was this most unique of American religious texts, the Book of Mormon, and its manuscripts. I am honored to be associated with the critical text project, and I thank Royal Skousen for granting me this privilege. ■

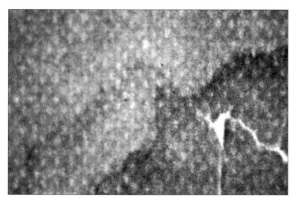

Paper A, fragments from 1 Nephi 14 through Jacob 4

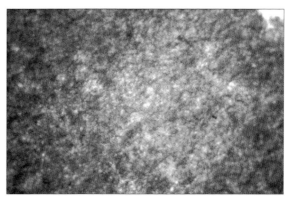

Paper B/D, fragments from Alma 10 through 3 Nephi 27

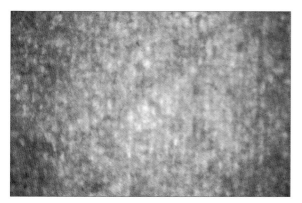

Paper C, fragments from Jacob 5 through Enos

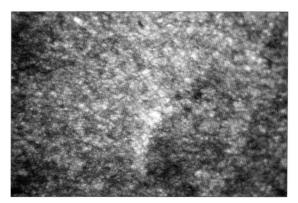

Paper E, fragments from the book of Ether

The four paper types of the Wilford Wood fragments of the original manuscript, magnified here 12 times.
Photographs by Robert Espinosa.

399 be established in this land & be set up as a free People by the Power of
of the Father that these might come forth from them unto a remnant of your
seed that the Covenant of the Father may be fulfiled which he hath coven
-anted with his People & House of Israel therefore when these works and
the work which shall be wrought among you hereafter shall come forth
from the Gentiles unto your seed which shall dwindle in unbelief be-
-cause of iniquity for thus it behoveth the Father that it should
come forth from the Gentiles that he may shew forth his power unto the
Gentiles for this cause, that the Gentiles if they will not harden their hearts
that they may repent and come unto me and be baptised in my name
and know of the true points of my doctrine that they may be numbered among
my People & House of Israel & when these things come to pass that thy seed
shall begin to know these things it shall be a sign unto them that they may
know that the work of the Father hath already commenced unto the fulfiling of
the Covenant which he hath made unto the People which are of the House of
Israel & when that day shall come it shall come to pass that Kings shall shut their mouths
for that which had not been told them shall they see & that which they had
not heard shall they consider, for in that day for my sake shall the Father
work a work which shall be a great & a marvelous work among them
and there shall be among them which will not believe it although a man
shall declare it unto them, but behold the life of my servant shall be in
my hand therefore they shall not hurt him although he shall be marred
because of them yet I will heal him for I will shew unto them that
my Wisdom is greater than the cunning of the Devil therefore it shall come
to pass that whosoever will not believe in my words which am Jesus Christ
which the Father shall cause him to bring forth unto the Gentiles & shall
give unto him power that he shall bring them forth unto the Gentiles
it shall be done even as Moses said they shall be cut off from among my
People which are of the Covenant & my People which are a remnant of Jacob
shall be among the Gentiles yea in the midst of them as a Lion among
the Beasts of the forest as a young Lion among the flocks of sheep who
if he go through both treadeth down & teareth in pieces & none can
deliver their hand shall be lifted up upon their adversaries & all their
Enemies shall be cut off yea woe be unto the Gentiles except they repent
for it shall come to pass in that day saith the Father that I will cut
off thy Horses out of the midst of thee & I will destroy thy Chariots & I will
cut off the cities of thy land & throw down all thy strong holds & I will cut
off witchcrafts out of thy hand & thou shalt have no more soothsayers thy
Graven Images I will also cut off & thy standing Images out of the midst

Color photograph of page 399 of the printer's manuscript (from 3 Nephi 21), photographed in October 1992 by Nevin Skousen.

The Printer's Manuscript

RONALD E. ROMIG

ROYAL SKOUSEN's initial contact with the Reorganized Church of Jesus Christ of Latter Day Saints (officially renamed the Community of Christ in April 2001) was in 1988 with Richard Howard, who at the time was the RLDS church historian. Richard made available a very good, high-quality copy of the printer's manuscript (called the copyflow) that Royal used to prepare his initial transcript of the manuscript. During that same year I accepted the position of archivist for the RLDS Church, but was unaware of the critical text project until Royal returned the copyflow of the printer's manuscript to us.

I assumed that with the return of the copyflow, our contact with Royal would be ended. Although I hoped that the results of his research would soon be in print, prior experience with people who want to pursue similar projects—making corrections in the Book of Mormon and perhaps printing a revised edition—had shown me that they quickly lost enthusiasm when they realized the magnitude of the project. And so I assumed the same would be true with this Royal Skousen from Utah. But everyone knows Royal is different.

Now that Royal's transcripts of the manuscripts are in print, it is fitting to recognize this remarkable accomplishment. Not only Royal, but his wife Sirkku and their family also merit credit—not only because they supported Royal's long-term commitment to this project, but also because Sirkku herself was a key participant in many aspects of the research.

In 1991, I began to grasp the scope of the critical text project. It was Royal's intention, using both the original and printer's manuscripts, to get as close as possible to the original text and to trace subsequent changes to the text. Royal had begun by making his transcripts from photographs of the original manuscript and from the copyflow of the printer's manuscript. If this was all that had been involved, I may have never met Royal, but he wished to be sure of some points by consulting the actual printer's manuscript. My most memorable experiences during my

The enlarged photocopy of the printer's manuscript (called the copyflow), loaned to the Book of Mormon critical text project in 1988. For size comparison, the photo also shows an original copy of the 1830 edition.

George Schweich displaying the printer's manuscript, which he inherited in 1888 at the death of his grandfather, David Whitmer. In 1903 Schweich sold the manuscript to the RLDS Church (officially renamed the Community of Christ in 2001).

tenure as church archivist are associated with the printer's manuscript of the Book of Mormon. Perhaps the most unforgettable occurred during the preparation for Royal and Sirkku's first visit to the library archives in April 1991.

In 1850, the printer's manuscript passed from Oliver Cowdery to David Whitmer, from whom George Schweich, Whitmer's grandson, received it in 1888. Schweich sold it to the RLDS Church in 1903. Since that time, the printer's manuscript had mostly been stored off-site from church headquarters in a bank vault in Kansas City. It was occasionally retrieved and placed on display. But, for the most part, even RLDS scholars had only had limited access to the actual manuscript. The church had made an effort to provide microfilm copies for scholarly use, including one copy for Brigham Young University in 1968, but access to the printer's manuscript itself was very limited. Once every decade we would get it out of the bank vault and have it on display one day during conference, and then it would be back in the vault for another decade.

When we first heard that Royal wanted to inspect the actual manuscript, you can imagine what this did to our view of how the manuscript should be handled. Nothing like this had ever happened in RLDS circles before. As the newly appointed church archivist and only having been employed in that position for a short time, it was a great responsibility having to make the arrangements to get this manuscript available

for research. It took no less than the direct participation of a member of the church's First Presidency, a member of the Presiding Bishopric (who is in charge of the financial affairs of the Community of Christ), Paul Edwards, the director of the Temple School (which had responsibility for the archives), and me. So together, we ceremoniously drove to Kansas City. The bishop, who had the key to the safe-deposit box, opened the box and handed the manuscript to the member of the First Presidency, who handed it to Paul Edwards, who handed it to me. We brought it back to Independence, and so we were ready when Royal and Sirkku arrived a few days later.

The presence of the manuscript was going to cause quite a bit of excitement, so we created a private work area in the library archives, at that time located in the auditorium, the large domed building across the street from the temple. Royal brought his transcription and began to examine the manuscript, comparing the transcript against the actual document. While he was doing that, Sirkku and I had the opportunity of doing a descriptive bibliography of the manuscript—measuring the leaves, including their thickness, and describing other characteristics of each page. Checking the transcription and doing the descriptive bibliography took two weeks.

Israel Smith, president of the RLDS Church and grandson of Joseph Smith Jr., viewing the printer's manuscript on display during the church's 1956 world conference.

In October 1992, the necessity for color photographs occasioned Royal's second visit to Independence. This time he was accompanied by his brother Nevin Skousen, who brought his own equipment with him. Because the printer's manuscript had never been photographed in color, this was another historic occasion. Nevin was an exceptionally skillful photographer and was perfectly matched for the important and challenging job of precisely filming the manuscript. Working together, we shot color negatives of the manuscript; it took two complete days to photograph the 466 pages of the manuscript.

While Nevin was having the film developed in Kansas City, Royal wanted to examine the entire collection of first-edition copies of the Book of Mormon in the RLDS library archives. These copies of the 1830 edition are stored off-site at the Church Records Center, so I had the task of transporting them from the repository to the library archives, where we were working. I will never forget the tension I felt during that drive from the records center to church headquarters, with more than twenty copies of the first edition on the back seat of my car. At that time each copy would have been conservatively valued at about $10,000. Royal completed his examination, and the books were returned to storage without incident.

Royal and Nevin then drove back to Utah, and two weeks later I flew to Utah with the negatives. We then worked two full days in Nevin's lab to create two sets of color prints from the negatives. Nevin used an enlarger to project each negative image onto photographic paper and then fed the exposed paper through his mini-photo lab. Each print took four minutes to travel through the machine. I tended the output rollers, separating the prints into two stacks as they emerged. The work was hot and largely done in the dark. Finally, Royal inspected the prints to ensure that each image was acceptable.

With this new research tool successfully created, I returned to Missouri, taking with me the negatives and one set of the color

A shelf filled with more than twenty copies of the first edition of the Book of Mormon, owned by the Community of Christ. These volumes were examined in 1992 and 1994 as part of the critical text project.

prints and leaving the other set in Royal's care. Subsequently, Royal helped the RLDS library archives acquire a refrigerator in which we now store the negatives to further ensure their long-term preservation.

In June 1994, Royal and Sirkku returned to the RLDS archives for a second detailed examination of the printer's manuscript. This time Royal checked for page rulings, finding that the spacing between the lines of text often varied from page to page. Sirkku and I checked pages for small scratches (or take marks) left by the 1830 compositor (that is, typesetter). Royal theorized that each time the compositor completed a stick of type, from 11 to 13 lines of type, he had marked his progress in the manuscript with a small impression, sometimes slightly cutting the paper. These marks are sometimes best discerned when viewed with a low-angle light.

While we worked on these take marks, Royal focused on corrections made in dark ink

Viewing the printer's manuscript and its transcript, at the end of two weeks' research on the manuscript, April 1991, Independence, Missouri: Royal Skousen, editor of the critical text project; archivist Ron Romig; and RLDS church historian Richard Howard, now emeritus.

found throughout the manuscript. These changes, nearly all grammatical, have traditionally been identified as the work of Joseph Smith when he edited the manuscript before printing the 1837 Kirtland edition. Using a hand microscope, Royal found that the ink in Joseph Smith's later corrections contains visible speckles, unlike the dark ink he used earlier on in his editing of the manuscript.

Doing research on the printer's manuscript, June 1994, Independence, Missouri: Ron Romig, archivist for the Community of Christ; Sirkku and Royal Skousen; and conservator Robert Espinosa.

During this 1994 visit, BYU conservator Robert Espinosa joined us to examine the paper types in the printer's manuscript. Robert identified eight different types of paper. All the papers are of the same basic size, referred to as "foolscap." One high-quality paper bears an O&H watermark. Three gatherings (9, 10, and 13) are composed of this paper. Four more gatherings (11, 15, 16, and 17) are from the same paper company but come from a different batch of paper and do not have the O&H watermark. Because of their high rag content, all the papers used for the printer's manuscript are in good condition.

Later that week, several visitors from LDS church headquarters in Salt Lake City came: Brian Reeves, an employee of the Historical Department; Richard Turley, director of the department; and Stephen Nadauld, the LDS church historian at that time. They brought samples of paper from the original (dictated) manuscript of the Book of Mormon. Robert continued his examination of the paper types by comparing the papers between the two manuscripts

and found that none of the papers in the printer's manuscript matched any of those from the original. Rick and Steve soon left, but Brian stayed and helped Sirkku and me in our continuing examination of the printer's manuscript. We were able to determine that there were no compositor's marks in gatherings 16 through 19 of the printer's manuscript, which confirmed Royal's belief that this portion of the manuscript was not used to set the type for the 1830 edition of the Book of Mormon. A possible explanation would be that scribes could not keep up in their copy work. Rather than slow up the printing, they let the compositor use the original manuscript to typeset this part of the text (from near the end of the book of Helaman to the end of Mormon).

After Robert and Brian returned to Utah, Royal paced himself for the rest of the week, examining specific details in the printer's manuscript, but restricting his time on each page to about three minutes in order to finish the task by the end of the week. By Friday morning, Sirkku and I had completed our list of take marks and Royal still had 100 pages left to examine, which he was able to finish by midday.

But in addition to completing his examination of the printer's manuscript, Royal wanted to see the 1830 editions again. And so I had the delightful opportunity to bring him 22 copies again from the records center. By that time, the value of each copy had increased to about $15,000. We lined them up on a vault shelf for Royal's review. Royal again checked for in-press changes made during the printing process. Variations between copies allowed him

Checking the paper types in the printer's manuscript, June 1994: Brian Reeves of the LDS Historical Department, Royal Skousen, and Robert Espinosa.

to identify the sequence of printing for many of the book's 37 gatherings.

Not only is Royal one of a handful of scholars to ever work directly with the printer's manuscript in its original format, he is also one of the last to work with it in that format. When obtained by the RLDS Church in 1903, the printer's manuscript was composed of large sheets of paper, each folded in half to make a folio of two leaves or four pages. Typically, six sheets were arranged into gatherings of 24 numbered pages. The manuscript thus was a stack of 21 gatherings, with the text reading from front to back like a book.

But soon after Royal's last visit (in 1994) and as a result of this critical text project, the printer's manuscript underwent conservation in Salt Lake City at the Historical Department there.

This conservation process lasted about six months and was done under the direction of Dale Heaps. The procedure was very detailed. First of all, we had to establish that the ink was insoluble, and then we were able to wash the leaves to remove the dirt, grime, and oil that had accumulated through the years. In another bath, we treated the leaves with deacidifying chemicals in order to prevent further deterioration

Findings about the Printer's Manuscript

1. For several of the gatherings, the typesetter cut the manuscript leaves in order to facilitate the typesetting. At some later time, these cut portions were pinned together in their correct order.

2. Some corrections were done immediately by the original scribe, some by a correcting scribe, some by the typesetter, and some considerably later by Joseph Smith (for the 1837 edition). In the printer's manuscript, Joseph Smith made over two thousand changes to the text by overwriting the original words or by crossing out words and inserting other words between the lines. These changes are mostly grammatical, but some involve clarification.

3. The scribes used a variety of paper types, with different thicknesses. Some of the sheets were lined in advance, others were lined by the scribe page by page as the copying took place. The watermark O&H is found on a handful of leaves.

4. The printer's manuscript does not contain any part of the original manuscript. The gatherings of the two manuscripts were never mixed up, even though for gatherings 16–19 of the printer's manuscript, the original manuscript was instead taken to the printer. In 3 Nephi 19 an unknown scribe (identified as scribe 2 of the printer's manuscript)

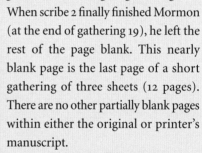

took over while Oliver Cowdery jumped ahead to start copying Ether (which begins gathering 20).

When scribe 2 finally finished Mormon (at the end of gathering 19), he left the rest of the page blank. This nearly blank page is the last page of a short gathering of three sheets (12 pages). There are no other partially blank pages within either the original or printer's manuscript.

5. Gatherings 16–19 of the printer's manuscript were not used by the printer. These gatherings show none of the typesetter's marks or corrections. This observation is confirmed by the presence of the typesetter's punctuation marks on corresponding fragments of the original manuscript.

6. Chapter specifications in the manuscripts are not original to the text. The chapter numbers were almost always added later. One of these chapter numbers (on page 261 of the printer's manuscript) is in blue ink rather than the normal black ink (now turned brown).

—Royal Skousen

above: *The original form of the printer's manuscript, a stack of 21 gatherings (each typically having six folded sheets), placed for size comparison in front of a facsimile 1830 edition.*

LEFT: *Washing a manuscript leaf to remove contaminants. Photograph by Dale Heaps.* RIGHT: *An entire sheet of the printer's manuscript, now encapsulated in Mylar.*

of the paper. After washing and deacidifying the leaves, Dale flattened them and reattached many of the leaves that had come apart—some had been cut during the typesetting of the 1830 edition. All those leaves were repaired and put back as far as possible into their original form. Finally, the leaves were encapsulated in Mylar. Dale also created a magnificent box in which the manuscript is now stored. Thus you have, in a sense, visual proof of the lasting legacy of the critical text project. While scholarly access to the manuscript is now possible, it is aesthetically an entirely different experience.

All these things might not have happened—the printer's manuscript might still be sitting in a bank vault in Kansas City—had Royal not been inspired to undertake this project. Royal's project has proven enormously significant. In addition to producing the definitive scholarly resource, Royal has forever changed the way we do Book of Mormon scholarship. His efforts have led to improved cooperation and extended contact between the LDS and the Community of Christ scholarly communities, and indeed the very way these religious institutions interact in the historical arena.

Book of Mormon Editions

LARRY W. DRAPER

I WAS employed in the Historical Department of the Church of Jesus Christ of Latter-day Saints for 18 years (until 1997). Earlier, as a graduate student at BYU, I worked as a student employee in Special Collections in the Harold B. Lee Library, where, among other assignments, I assisted Chad Flake with his Mormon bibliography during the years 1976–78; this monumental bibliography was published in 1978. I mention this because the work I did for Chad partially prepared me to assume the role of the rare book librarian at the Historical Department when Don Schmidt retired in 1985. I took that position during those sad days of the Mark Hofmann forgeries and bombs.

I met Royal Skousen in 1988 when it became my job to give Royal access to copies of various editions of the Book of Mormon so that he could do the necessary analysis of the text as it changed from edition to edition. We provided copies of at least thirteen different editions (1837, 1840, 1849, 1852, 1858 Wright, 1874 RLDS, 1879, 1888 large print, 1902, 1905, 1906 large print, 1911, and 1920). In most cases these copies were scanned at the Humanities Research Center at BYU and thus put into electronic form, which has facilitated analysis of textual changes.

We glean information about the printed editions of the Book of Mormon mainly from these sources:

(1) accounts of what happened, either in
manuscript or in published form

(2) knowledge of the physical methods of
the printing process (in other words,
how the printing was actually done on
a printing press)

(3) actual evidence left behind in copies of
the books

Most of the time, one source will confirm information from another source—for example, when a published account of what happened for a particular edition agrees with the physical evidence presented by a copy of the book. Occasionally one source of information will disagree with another and we arrive at an unexpected conclusion, as the following cases will demonstrate.

The Unbound Sheets of the 1830 Edition

A study of the printing history of the Book of Mormon first requires an examination of the unbound sheets of the 1830 edition. These sheets were acquired by Wilford Wood, a furrier from Bountiful, Utah. Later the sheets came into the possession of the Historical Department, where they are housed today.

We learn several interesting things by examining these sheets. One is that John Gilbert's description of the printing of the 1830 edition is essentially accurate, even though the account was written sixty-three years after the event.[1] We also learn that the unbound sheets are not proof sheets (as had been claimed). Except for the last sheet (gathering 37), there is no evidence that these sheets were used as proof sheets. Nor is there any evidence that they were the first copies to come off the press (as had also been claimed). Rather, the evidence shows that these sheets are "throwaways"—that is, sheets that had flaws which made them unacceptable for a bound book, and they were therefore removed from the pile of usable sheets.

Gilbert states that the 1830 edition was "printed 16 pages at a time, so that one sheet of paper made two copies of 16 pages each, requiring 2500 sheets of paper for each form of 16 pages. There were 37 forms of 16 pages each."[2] So what does that mean? It means that the book was printed using the "work and turn" (or half-sheet imposition) method, where each side of a sheet was printed from one form of type with one pull of the press—that is, 2500 sheets of large paper that, following the printing of both sides, were cut in half to create five thousand half-sheets.[3] Wilford Wood's unbound sheets are a complete set of these half-sheets, one for each of the book's 37 gatherings. The originally larger sheet was folded in half and cut down the center with a bone cutter to create two half-sheets. The resulting half-sheets therefore have one rough edge on one of their longer sides. Louis Crandall, proprietor of the Crandall Historical Printing Museum in Provo and a printer by trade, came up to the Historical Department to help with the examination of the unbound sheets. He suggested that we look for pinholes along the roughly cut edge of each half-sheet. These pinholes should be there if the printer had used the "work and turn" method. And indeed, we did find pinholes on the unbound half-sheets. The pinholes resulted from two pins (called points) piercing the full sheet when the first side of the sheet was printed. The pinholes allowed the printer, when printing the second side of the sheet, to correctly place the sheet so that the printed text on both sides would be properly aligned (or registered).

Thus the unbound sheets that Wilford Wood acquired confirm John Gilbert's description of how the Book of Mormon was printed in 1829–30. This

Printing a gathering of 16 pages

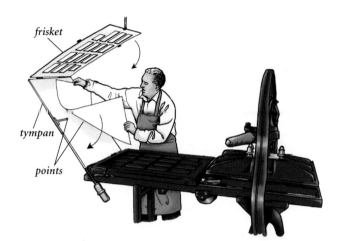

1 *To print the first side (the "iteration" process), the sheet is placed on the tympan and positioned against a horizontal and vertical set of guides. The lower horizontal guides (called "duck bills") position the paper level. The sheet is centered by means of the vertical guide. The frisket is lowered down over the sheet to hold it against the tympan.*

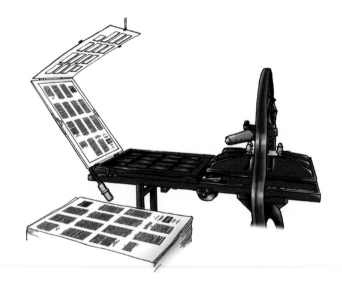

4 *The bed of type with the tympan and frisket is slid back out. The tympan and frisket assembly, with the frisket holding the sheet tight against the tympan, is then lifted from the inked type. The frisket is raised and the printed sheet is removed from the points and placed on a table to dry.*

for the 1830 edition of the Book of Mormon

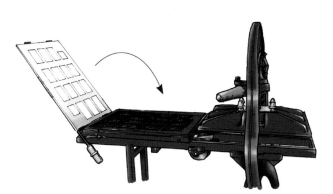

2 *The form is inked by using ink balls, and then the tympan and frisket with the positioned sheet are lowered down on top of the bed of type.*

3 *The bed is slid under the platen. The pressman gives a strong pull, allowing the platen bearers to ensure an even pressure over the entire bed of type and to drive the two pinlike points through the sheet of paper.*

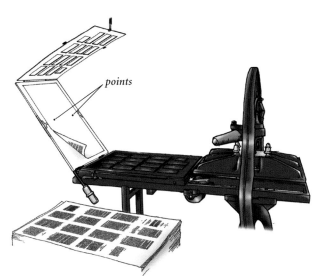

points

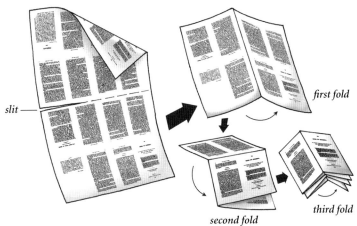

slit

first fold

second fold

third fold

5 *When printing the second side of the sheet (the "re-iteration" process), the sheet is rotated head to foot, then placed on the tympan so that the points enter the pinholes made in the iteration. Steps 2 through 4 are then repeated. This "work and turn" process reduces by half the required number of impositions.*

6 *The completely printed sheet can now be slit into two half-sheets. Each half is then folded three times to make a "gathering" of 16 pages.*

imposition arrangement also explains the patterns of in-press changes for some of the gatherings. Early on in the printing of a given sheet, the typesetter might find a few typos in that sheet and would have the pressmen stop so that these typos could be corrected.

Stereotyping: The 1840 Cincinnati/Nauvoo Edition

The printing method known as *stereotyping* was first used around 1799. It is a process of creating printing plates from a typeset form of moveable type. Stereotyping serves at least two purposes. It allows the printer or the publisher to print small print runs (say a thousand copies or less at different times at one, two, or even twenty year intervals, if desired) without having to reset the type each time. It also allows the original moveable type to immediately be used again for a different task (for instance, setting a new type form for a different gathering of the same book or for a different book) while the actual printing of the earlier sheet is being done with

the stereotype. There are, however, disadvantages. The printer cannot easily correct mistakes of typesetting (as can be done with the non-plate printing method) because each letter is not a single piece of type. So in-press changes like those that are common in the 1830 edition, and to a lesser extent in the 1837 edition, are not easily made.

The first use of stereotype plates for printing the Book of Mormon was the 1840 edition. With the use of stereotype plates, a new term regarding Book of Mormon printing makes its appearance: *impression,* meaning "printing." The previous editions, 1830 and 1837, are correctly referred to as *editions,* but with the 1840 publication of the Book of Mormon using stereotype plates, we must be more specific and refer to subsequent printings using these plates as *impressions* or *printings.* This terminology has caused some confusion, because often the words *edition* and *printing* (that is, *impression*) are incorrectly interchanged.

The 1840 edition is known in four different impressions made from plates that were stereotyped in Cincinnati, Ohio. The printing of the first impression

Stereotyping a typeset page

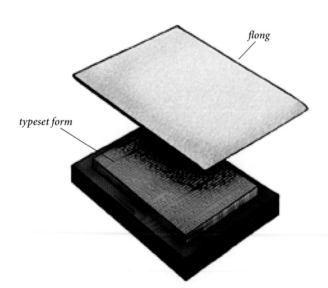

1 *A moist sheet of papier-mâché (called a "flong") is pressed down upon the original typeset form to create an impression of the original type.*

2 *When the flong has dried, it is placed into a hollow metal frame and covered with a lid. The frame is then screwed tightly together and tilted up vertically.*

was begun even before the final stereotype (of the last gathering) was made. That is one of the beauties of the stereotype method. You can be working on the next typesetting project while printing from the new plates. The first printing of the 1840 edition did take place in Cincinnati (although the title page indicates it was published in Nauvoo), and by October of 1840, two thousand copies were bound and in hand. So the 1840 Nauvoo edition could correctly be called the 1840 Cincinnati impression (published in Nauvoo but printed in Cincinnati).

The plates were then taken to Nauvoo, where in the spring of 1841, a new impression of "several hundred copies" was run. A third impression was probably done in early 1842, as suggested by an advertisement in the January and February 1842 issues of the church's newspaper *Times and Seasons*. Keep in mind that these three impressions all have Nauvoo and 1840 on the title page. They are distinguished as different impressions by a change in the arrangement of the witness pages at the end of the book (pp. 572, 573, and 574). They are also differentiated by a broken

3 *Molten metal is now poured into the tightened frame to create a precise cast of the original typeset form. When the metal cools, the resulting stereotype is used in the press just like the original typeset form.*

letter and a variation in the paper type. A fourth impression using these stereotype plates was run in Nauvoo in August 1842, with two changes on the title page: the date was changed from 1840 to 1842, and the Jr. from Joseph Smith's name was dropped because Joseph Smith Sr. had died in September of 1840.

This 1842 impression is also of note because it is much more rare than any of the previous editions or printings of the Book of Mormon. Probably only 640 copies were printed, and few have survived compared to the copies left from the three earlier impressions (of about four thousand printed copies).[4]

The pattern of printing from stereotype plates was now set and would be used time and time again in printing later editions.

1852 Liverpool Edition

The 1852 Liverpool edition was also a stereotype. In his early examinations of this edition in the Historical Department, Royal discovered a second copy that had textual differences from the first 1852 copy. These textual differences were puzzling at first because we did not know how stereotype plates could be "corrected." It was later discovered that Franklin Richards, at that time president of the British Mission, and his brother Samuel W. Richards did make corrections to the 1852 stereotype. Some were minor corrections in punctuation, but textual corrections were also made by referencing the 1840 edition. However, this use of the 1840 edition was omitted for some gatherings, with the result that the famous "white and delightsome" phrase from 2 Nephi 30:6 (the earliest extant reading) did not reappear in the LDS text as "pure and delightsome" until the 1981 edition. (By the way, there are only two known copies of the corrected 1852 impression; we only have an uncorrected copy at BYU.)

A brief word on how stereotype plates are corrected may be of interest. Further study of the stereotype method of printing taught us that stereotype plates were commonly corrected. This is done by shaving the offending letter (or letters) off the plate with a chisel-like tool. This can be done because the plates are made of lead, which is relatively soft. Then a hole is drilled through the plate at the spot where the letter was removed and a single piece of regular type—the correct letter, of course—is placed in the hole, set at the proper height, and soldered into place so that it will not move during printing. Thus corrections to the stereotype plates can and did occur on

a regular basis, although it was much more difficult and time-consuming than with moveable type. Sometimes the corrections were made with pieces of type that did not match the original font, resulting in very obvious and even awkward looking corrections.

The 1852 Liverpool stereotyped edition was the beginning of a long line of impressions: the original uncorrected 1852 followed by the 1852 corrected, two more impressions in 1854, and then the 1866. Sometime in 1870, the plates were shipped from Liverpool to Salt Lake City, thus beginning a series of impressions made in Utah, from 1871 up to 1877.

The printing history of the Book of Mormon is indeed interesting and instructive. I am glad that Royal Skousen began this project and did a proper study and that it is finally nearing completion. I look forward to his later volume on the analysis on the printed editions. I am happy to have had a small part in this project. ■

The 1852 Stereotyped Edition

IMPRESSION	PLACE	STATED EDITION	DATE ON TITLE PAGE
First	Liverpool	Third European	1852
Second	Liverpool	Third European[5]	1852
Third	Liverpool	Fourth European	1854
Fourth	Liverpool	Fifth European[6]	1854
Fifth	Liverpool	Sixth European[7]	1866
Sixth	Salt Lake City		1871
Seventh	Salt Lake City		1874
Eighth	Salt Lake City		1876
Ninth	Salt Lake City		1877

NOTES

1. See Royal Skousen, "John Gilbert's 1892 Account of the 1830 Printing of the Book of Mormon," in *The Disciple as Witness: Essays on Latter-day Saint History and Doctrine in Honor of Richard Lloyd Anderson,* ed. Stephen D. Ricks, Donald W. Parry, and Andrew H. Hedges (Provo, Utah: FARMS, 2000). A transcription of Gilbert's account appears on pages 400–405.

2. Skousen, "Gilbert's 1892 Account," 397.

3. Skousen, "Gilbert's 1892 Account," 397. See Peter Crawley, *A Descriptive Bibliography of the Mormon Church. Volume One, 1830–1847* (Provo, Utah: BYU Religious Studies Center, 1997), 379 n. 9.

4. For a discussion of the Cincinnati and Nauvoo impressions, see Crawley, entry 83, pp. 129–33, and entry 159, p. 205.

5. This is the 1852 corrected impression. It includes the attribution "Moroni" at the foot of the text on the title page, which was taken from the 1840 edition.

6. The attribution "Moroni" was dropped from the foot of the text on the title page.

7. Hugh Stocks asserts that in addition to the obvious impressions listed here, there was an additional impression, which he dates to about 1870, but which is dated 1866 on the title page. Stocks also asserts the plates were sent to Salt Lake City around 1870, which allowed the beginning of a new series of American impressions. See Hugh G. Stocks, "The Book of Mormon, 1830–1879: A Publishing History" (master's thesis, University of California at Los Angeles, 1979), 97–105.

The Systematic Text of the Book of Mormon

ROYAL SKOUSEN

In my initial work on the original manuscript of the Book of Mormon, I was always excited to discover the occasional error that had crept into the text. But over time I have become more amazed about the nature of the original English-language text of the Book of Mormon.

One aspect of the text that has surprised me is the internal consistency of the original text. (For the meaning of the term *original text,* see the discussion on page 5.) Occasionally a mistake in transcription or printing has introduced a reading into the text that is inconsistent with all other usage in the Book of Mormon. Even some cases of editing have led to such inconsistency. These changes do not affect the message or doctrine of the Book of Mormon, but it has been marvelous to see just how consistent the original text was.

In this paper, I will provide evidence for 56 proposed textual changes in the Book of Mormon. The term *textual change* means an alteration in the words or phrases of a passage or a consistent change in the spelling of a name. Of these proposed changes, 38 are textually significant, but only in the sense that they would also show up when translating the text into other languages. On the other hand, 18 of the changes involve minor variation in the phraseology of the text. These changes do not involve any significant change in meaning. Nonetheless, these minor errors show how consistent the original text was, even in its phraseology. The language of the original text was very tightly controlled.

Consistency in Meaning

I begin this paper by discussing a good number of textual changes which show that the semantically better (or more appropriate) reading is found in the earliest textual source—usually the original manuscript, but sometimes in the printer's manuscript when the original manuscript is no longer extant. The symbol $\mathcal{O}$ will be used to stand for the original manuscript; and $\mathcal{P}$ will stand for the printer's manuscript, the copy of $\mathcal{O}$ that the scribes prepared for the printer of the first edition (1830, Palmyra, New York).

Editions are identified by the year in which they were published (from the 1830 edition to the 1981 LDS edition). Unless otherwise noted, Book of Mormon passages and names will be cited as they are found in the earliest textual sources.

■ *The devil is the proprietor, not preparator, of hell.*

> 1 Nephi 15:35   and there is a place prepared
>   yea even that awful hell of which I have spoken
>   and the devil is the **proprietor** of it

> > *propriator:* scribe 2's original spelling of *proprietor* in Ⓞ
> >
> > *preparator:* Oliver Cowdery's interpretation, in Ⓟ; followed by 1830 and 1981
> >
> > *father:* Joseph Smith's first emendation, in Ⓟ
> >
> > *foundation:* Joseph Smith's second emendation, also in Ⓟ; followed by 1837 and all subsequent editions except for 1981

In the original manuscript, scribe 2's *prepriator* is quite unusual, especially his spelling of the first (unstressed) vowel as *e* rather than *o.* Oliver Cowdery misinterpreted the word as *preparator,* a virtually nonexistent word in English; according to the Oxford English Dictionary, a preparator is a preparer of medicines or specimens. Oliver was probably influenced by the earlier occurrence in this verse of the word *prepared.* The difficulty of the word *preparator* explains Joseph Smith's varying attempts to come up with a better reading for the 1837 edition (first, *father,* then *foundation*). The devil as proprietor (or owner and operator) of hell makes very good sense. (Renee Bangerter first suggested this reading as a conjectural emendation.)

■ *The wicked are separated, not rejected, from the righteous and the tree of life.*

> 1 Nephi 15:36   wherefore the wicked are **separated** from the righteous
>   and also from that tree of life

> > *seperated:* scribe 2's spelling of *separated* in Ⓞ
> >
> > *rejected:* Oliver Cowdery's misreading, in Ⓟ; followed by 1830 and all subsequent editions

Oliver Cowdery miscopied scribe 2's *seperated* as the visually similar *rejected.* Elsewhere in the Book of Mormon text, people can be separated as a result of sin and judgment. Note in particular the usage in nearby verse 28: "it was an awful gulf which separateth the wicked from the tree of life and also from the saints of God." We get the same meaning as in verse 36: the wicked are separated from the righteous saints of God and from the tree of life.

■ *Alma did know about the persecutors of the church.*

> Mosiah 26:9   and it came to pass that Alma **did know** concerning them
>   **for** there were many witnesses against them

> > *did know ... for:* original reading in Ⓟ, in scribe 2's hand; Ⓞ not extant
> >
> > *did not know ... for:* Oliver Cowdery's later correction, also in Ⓟ; followed by 1830 and most subsequent editions
> >
> > *did not know ... but:* 1920 emendation; followed by 1981

The unknown scribe 2 of the printer's manuscript originally wrote "Alma did know concerning them / for there were many witnesses against them," a reading which makes perfectly good sense. Oliver Cowdery later corrected the text here by inserting the word *not*, perhaps because of the unusualness of the paraphrastic *did* in the verb phrase "did know." This emendation resulted in a difficult reading, which was somewhat alleviated in the 1920 edition by substituting *but* for the conjunction *for*. The earliest reading (in scribe 2's hand in the printer's manuscript) is precisely correct.

■ *The queen clapped, not clasped, her hands.*

Alma 19:30   and when she had said this
                    she **clapped** her hands
                    being filled with joy

> *claped:* Oliver Cowdery's spelling in 𝒫 for *clapped*; 𝒪 not extant; recent RLDS editions have *clapped*

> *clasped:* 1830 misreading; followed by most subsequent editions

The 1830 typesetter apparently interpreted Oliver Cowdery's spelling *claped* as missing an *s*, yet this spelling is simply the result of the scribes' tendency to not double consonants after a short vowel. Elsewhere, the text does refer to the more emotional clapping of hands ("they clapped their hands for joy," in Mosiah 18:11), but never to clasping hands. In this second example, Oliver Cowdery also spelled *clapped* with a single *p*.

■ *Repentance involves both acknowledging faults and repairing wrongs.*

Alma 39:12–13   therefore I command you my son in the fear of God . . .
                    that ye lead away the hearts of no more to do wickedly
                    but rather return unto them and acknowledge your faults
                    and **repair** that wrong which ye have done

> *acknowledge your faults and **repair** that wrong:* reading in 𝒪, in Oliver Cowdery's hand; accidental ink drop on the *p* of *repair*

> *acknowledge your faults and **retain** that wrong:* Oliver Cowdery's misreading, in 𝒫; followed by 1830 and most subsequent editions

> *acknowledge your faults and that wrong:* 1920 emendation; followed by 1981

The original manuscript reads *repair*, but sometime before the text was copied into the printer's manuscript, a number of ink drops fell on this page. One fell right on the *p* of *repair* and looks like a crossing on the ascender of the *p*. Since Oliver Cowdery's *r*'s and *n*'s frequently look alike, the resulting word looks like *retain*, which is how Oliver Cowdery copied the word. The use of *retain* in this passage doesn't make sense, thus in the 1920 edition the word was simply deleted. The original reading here ("repair that wrong") is consistent with other Book of Mormon passages that refer to repentance—as in Mosiah 27:35, where the sons of Mosiah were "zealously striving to repair all the injuries which they had done to the church / confessing all their sins / and publishing all the things which they had seen." (Similar language is found in Alma 27:8 and Helaman 5:17.)

■ *The Nephite dissenters almost outnumbered the Nephites.*

Alma 43:13–14   and thus the Nephites were compelled alone
       to withstand against the Lamanites
       which were a compound of Laman and Lemuel
          and the sons of Ishmael
       and all those which had dissented from the Nephites
       which were Amlicites and Zoramites
          and the descendants of the priests of Noah
       now those **dissenters** were as numerous nearly as were the Nephites

desenters: Oliver Cowdery's spelling in 𝓞 for *dissenters*

desendants: Oliver Cowdery's spelling in 𝓟 for *descendants* (a misreading of 𝓞)

descendants: spelling in 1830 and all subsequent editions, following 𝓟

Oliver Cowdery miscopied *dissenters* (spelled *desenters*) as *descendants* (spelled *desendants*). The previous verse lists all the Nephite dissenters, ending up with "the descendants of the priests of Noah," yet quite clearly in a few generations the descendants of a couple dozen priests could never have increased to almost equal the population of the entire (non-dissenting) Nephite nation.

■ *The Lamanites had only one second leader, not several.*

Alma 47:13   . . . and that he would deliver them up into Lehonti's hands
       if he would make him Amalickiah
       the second leader over the whole army

the second leader: reading in 𝓞, in Oliver Cowdery's hand

a second leader: miscopied by Oliver Cowdery in 𝓟; followed by 1830 and all subsequent editions

Oliver Cowdery miscopied *the* as the indefinite article *a*. This error occurred because the definite article *the* was at the end of the line and was therefore easily misread. As explained later on in the story, there was only one second leader (thus Alma 47:17: "if their chief leader was killed / to appoint the second leader to be their chief leader").

■ *Moroni asked Parhoron to heed, not read, his petition.*

Alma 51:15   he sent a petition with the voice of the people
       unto the governor of the land
       desiring that he should **heed** it
       and give him Moroni power to compel those dissenters

head: Oliver Cowdery's spelling for *heed* in 𝓞, also his corrected spelling in 𝓟

read: 1830 printer's misinterpretation of *head*, marked in pencil in 𝓟; followed by 1830 and all subsequent editions

Oliver Cowdery frequently spells *heed* as *head* (for instance, in the original manuscript for Alma 49:30: "because of their head & diligence"). The 1830 typesetter was usually able to correctly interpret this particular misspelling. But in Alma 51:15 he could not understand "he should head it." He thought the word *head* was an error for *read,* and thus he overwrote (in pencil) the initial *h* with an *r.* The use of *heed,* of course, makes perfectly good sense, but requesting Parhoron to read the petition does sound quite unnecessary.

Systematic Phraseology

I now turn to examples where the phraseology of the original text is strongly supported by all other usage in the Book of Mormon. Each error described in this section has led to a "wrinkle" in the text. Nonetheless, these textual errors have not been found except by discovering the correct reading in the manuscripts.

■ *Multitudes are always pressing, not feeling, their way forward.*

> 1 Nephi 8:31   and he also saw other multitudes **pressing** their way
> towards that great and spacious building

> *prſsing:* scribe 3's spelling in 𝒪 of *pressing* (that is, without the *e*)

> *feeling:* Oliver Cowdery's misreading, in 𝒫; followed by 1830 and all subsequent editions

There are no scriptural uses of "feeling one's way." Here in the original manuscript scribe 3 wrote *prſsing* (where *ſ* stands for an elongated *s*). Scribe 3's initial *p* looks like an *f*, so when Oliver Cowdery copied the text into the printer's manuscript, he misread *pressing* as *feeling.* Similar descriptions in Lehi's dream also use *press* rather than *feel:*

> 1 Nephi 8:21   and I saw numberless concourses of people
> many of whom were *pressing* forward

> 1 Nephi 8:24   I beheld others *pressing* forward . . .
> and they did *press* forward

> 1 Nephi 8:30   he saw other multitudes *pressing* forward . . .
> and they did *press* their way forward

There are other uses of "press forward" in 2 Nephi 31:20 and Ether 14:12. (Lyle Fletcher first discovered this change of *pressing* to *feeling.*)

■ *The justice of God is a sword.*

> 1 Nephi 12:18   and a great and a terrible gulf divideth them
> yea even the **sword** of the justice of the eternal God

> *sword:* reading in 𝒪, in scribe 2's hand

> *word:* Oliver Cowdery's miscopying of *sword* as *word* in 𝒫; followed by 1830 and all subsequent editions

In the original manuscript, scribe 2's initial *s* looks like an undotted *i*, which led Oliver Cowdery to accidentally misread *sword* as *word* when he copied this passage into the printer's manuscript. There are no other examples of "the word of justice" in the Book of Mormon text, but there are seven other examples of "the sword of justice":

> Alma 26:19   the sword of his justice
>
> Alma 60:29   the sword of justice
>
> Helaman 13:5   the sword of justice (2 times)
>
> 3 Nephi 20:20   the sword of my justice
>
> 3 Nephi 29:4   the sword of his justice
>
> Ether 8:23   the sword of the justice of the eternal God

The last example is precisely the same as the original reading in 1 Nephi 12:18.

Minor Wrinkles in the Current Text

In this section, I list 12 different cases where the phraseology in the original text was perfectly consistent, but over the years occasional printing errors have led to exceptions in the phraseology. These errors do not lead to any substantive change in meaning. But these wrinkles do show just how consistent the original text was, even in cases of minor phraseology.

■ *this time*, never *these times* when referring to present time

> original text: 61 to 0
> current text: 60 to 1

> > 1 Nephi 10:19
> > > as well in **this time** as in times of old and as well in times of old as in times to come > **these times** (1830)
> > > [Note the influence of the plural *times* for past and future.]

■ *whatsoever*, never *whatever*

> original text: 74 to 0
> current text: 72 to 2

> > Jacob 1:11
> > > let them be of **whatsoever** name they would > **whatever** (1830)

> > Helaman 3:5
> > > in **whatsoever** parts it had not been rendered desolate > **whatever** (1830)

■ *to do iniquity*, never *to do iniquities*

> original text: 22 to 0
> current text: 21 to 1

> > Jacob 2:35
> > > ye have done greater **iniquity** than the Lamanites > **iniquities** (1830)

■ *to have hope*, never *to have hoped*

> original text: 18 to 0
> current text: 17 to 1

> > Jacob 5:46
> > > and these **I had hope** to preserve > **had hoped** (1837)
> > > [Joseph Smith's editing in the printer's manuscript; in-press change in the 1837 edition]

■ *if it so be that*, never *if it be so that*

> original text: 38 to 0
> current text: 36 to 2

> > Jacob 5:64
> > > and if it **so be** that these last grafts shall grow > **be so** (1852)

> > Ether 2:20
> > > and if it **so be** that the water come in upon thee > **be so** (1849)

■ *the Nephites and the Lamanites,* never *the Nephites and Lamanites*

> original text: 15 to 0
> current text: 14 to 1

>> Enos 1:24
>>> and I saw wars between the Nephites and **the** Lamanites > **NULL** (1830)
>>> [NULL means that one or more words have been deleted.]

■ *to observe to keep the commandments,* never *to observe the commandments*

> original text: 11 to 0
> current text: 10 to 1

>> Mosiah 4:30
>>> and observe **to keep** the commandments of God > **NULL** (1837)

■ *to set a mark upon someone,* never *to set a mark on someone*

> original text: 9 to 0
> current text: 8 to 1

>> Alma 3:14
>>> and I will set a mark **upon** them > **on** (1837)

■ *thus ended a period of time,* never *thus endeth a period of time* (usually a year)

> original text: 47 to 0
> current text: 43 to 4

>> Alma 3:27
>>> and thus **ended** the fifth year > **endeth** (1830)
>> Alma 28:7
>>> and thus **ended** the fifteenth year > **endeth** (1837)
>> Alma 51:37
>>> and thus **ended** the twenty and fifth year > **endeth** (1849)
>> Alma 51:37
>>> and thus **ended** the days of Amalickiah > **endeth** (1849)

■ *to meet a person,* never *to meet with a person*

> original text: 51 to 0
> current text: 50 to 1

>> Alma 17:1
>>> he met ^ the sons of Mosiah > **with** (1830)

■ *conditions,* never *condition*

> original text: 14 to 0
> current text: 12 to 2

>> Alma 27:24
>>> and we will guard them from their enemies by our armies on **conditions**
>>> that they will give us a portion of their substance > **condition** (1920)
>>>> [change marked in the 1920 committee copy (1911 Chicago edition)]
>> Helaman 14:18
>>> yea and it bringeth to pass the **conditions** of repentance > **condition** (1830)

■ *into one's hands,* never *unto one's hands*

> original text: 56 to 0
> current text: 55 to 1
>> Alma 57:12
>>> therefore they yielded up the city **into** our hands > **unto** (1920)
>>>> [change not marked in the 1920 committee copy (1911 Chicago edition)]

Increased Parallelism

Frequently the original text shows a higher degree of parallelism between its linguistic elements. In the following example, the parallelism of the original text is assured by repeating a linguistic element (in this case, the preposition).

■ *There was rejoicing among the relatives of Parhoron and also among the people of liberty.*

> Alma 51:7   and Parhoron retained the judgment seat
> which caused much rejoicing among the brethren of Parhoron
> and also **among the people** of liberty
>
> ***among the people:*** reading in ℗, in Oliver Cowdery's hand
>
> ***many the people:*** Oliver Cowdery's miscopying of *among* as *many* in ℗
>
> ***many of the people:*** John Gilbert's correction in ℗ (*of* added in pencil); followed by 1830 and all subsequent editions

The original text here shows parallelism by repeating the preposition *among* ("among X and also among Y"). Oliver Cowdery misread the second *among* as *many*. John Gilbert, the 1830 typesetter, realized that "many the people" was not acceptable, so he inserted the preposition *of*.

Punctuation and Parallelism

As far as we can determine, the original text of the Book of Mormon had no punctuation. The original manuscript had some dashes in the summaries that are typically found at the beginning of books or sections of books, but elsewhere in the original manuscript the scribes provided no punctuation. For the printer's manuscript, Oliver Cowdery and scribe 2 added some punctuation as they copied the original manuscript. The 1830 typesetter, John Gilbert, ignored the scribes' suggested punctuation and provided his own as he set the type. In most instances, Gilbert's punctuation (or its equivalent) has been retained in the text. In some cases, later editors of the text have emended his punctuation. Even so, there are still a few cases where there is good reason to further emend the punctuation. In the following example, we see that the punctuation should probably be changed in order to maintain the parallel nature of the original text.

■ *The life of the soul is eternal.*

> Alma 42:16–17   now repentance could not come unto men
> except there were a punishment
> —which also was as eternal as the life of **the soul**—
> **should be affixed** opposite to the plan of happiness
> which was as eternal also as the life of the soul /
> now how could a man repent except he should sin . . .

The 1830 typesetter incorrectly placed the punctuation after "should be" (although in the printer's manuscript he correctly marked the punctuation as coming before "should be"). All subsequent editions have followed his final decision to make the break right before the word *affixed*. But the resulting parenthetical clause claims that there must be a punishment that is as eternal "as the life of the soul should be"—which really doesn't make much sense. The life of the soul "is eternal," not "should be eternal." Alma is saying that "a punishment . . . should be affixed opposite to the plan of happiness"—a plan which should correspondingly be "as eternal also as the life of the soul." Notice that at the end of the verse the punctuation must occur at the end of the phrase "the life of the soul."

Agreement with the King James Version

The Book of Mormon sometimes quotes from the King James Version (KJV) of the Bible. In many cases a change has taken the text away from its original reading, which happens to be the same as the reading in the KJV.

■ *The Lord will break the Assyrians in the land of Israel.*

> 2 Nephi 24:25　　　. . . that I will **break** the Assyrian in my land
> 　　　　　　　　　　and upon my mountains tread him under foot
>
> > **break:** reading in Ⓞ, in Oliver Cowdery's hand; same reading in KJV
> >
> > **bring:** Oliver Cowdery's miscopying of *break* as *bring* in Ⓟ; followed by 1830 and all subsequent editions

The KJV for Isaiah 14:25 reads *break* ("I will break the Assyrian in my land"), as does the original manuscript of the Book of Mormon. The word *break* was hyphenated at the end of a line, so that the final *k* was placed at the beginning of the next line. In his copy work, Oliver Cowdery misread the *brea* at the end of the line as the beginning of the word *bring*. The change to *bring* obscures the original semantic parallelism in this verse (where both clauses refer to the destruction of the Assyrian army within the borders of Israel).

Name Changes

In this section, I discuss two interesting cases where the manuscript evidence supports a change in the spelling of a Book of Mormon name. In both of these cases, the original spelling reveals an interesting aspect regarding the history of the peoples in the Book of Mormon.

■ *Muloch,* not *Mulek*

> The earliest manuscript spelling for the surviving son of king Zedekiah reads *Muloch* (in Mosiah 25:2 of the printer's manuscript). On the other hand, this name is spelled *Mulek* in Helaman 6–8 of the printer's manuscript. This alternative spelling is probably due to the nearby influence of 13 occurrences of the name of the city *Mulek* (consistently spelled as such in both manuscripts, from Alma 51 through Helaman 5). Note that the spelling *Muloch* suggests an ominous connection with the god *Molech/Moloch* (to which children in Israel were sacrificed prior to the Babylonian captivity—see 1 Kings 11:7–8, 2 Kings 23:10, and Acts 7:43).

■ *Amlicites,* not *Amalekites*

There is only one group of dissenters that Amlici founded—namely, the Amlicites, first described in Alma 2–3. This same dissident group is later referred to (in the current text) as the Amalekites (Alma 21–27, 43). But the earliest extant manuscript spelling (in Alma 24:1) spells the name of this "other" group as *Amelicites,* with only the one vowel difference between *Amlicites* and *Amelicites.* The incorrect later spelling *Amalekites* may have been influenced by the competing name *Amaleki,* which in the Book of Mormon refers to the record keeper first mentioned in Omni 1:12 or one of the men of Ammon listed in Mosiah 7:6. Another possible source for the secondary spelling is the Amalekites, a prominent people in the land of Canaan and frequently mentioned in the Old Testament.

Original Lack of Redundancy

We sometimes find that errors have created unnecessary redundancies, as in the following example.

■ *You would behold quickly.*

Alma 33:21   if ye could be healed by merely casting about your eyes
                 that ye might **behold**
         would ye not behold quickly

     behold: reading in 𝓞, in Oliver Cowdery's hand; the *o* is no longer extant

     be healed: Oliver Cowdery's misreading, in 𝓟; followed by 1830 and all subsequent editions

Oliver Cowdery wrote *beh* at the end of the line in the original manuscript, then *-old* at the beginning of the next line (although the line-initial hyphen and the *o* are no longer extant). When copying into the printer's manuscript, Oliver Cowdery accidentally misread the hyphenated word as *be healed.* The emphasis in this passage is on beholding quickly. There is no need to repeat the already stated condition of being healed as the text now redundantly reads "if ye could be *healed* by merely casting about your eyes that ye might be *healed.*"

Variation in the Text

When emending the text, it is important to keep in mind that not every case of variation in the text should be made consistent. There will exist legitimate possibilities of choice involving alternative phraseology or semantically similar words.

■ *Moroni was appointed chief commander.*

Alma 43:17   and he was only twenty and five years old
            when he was appointed **chief commander**
            over the armies of the Nephites

     chief commander: reading in 𝓞, in Oliver Cowdery's hand; 1830 follows 𝓞 rather than 𝓟

     chief captain: Oliver Cowdery's substitution, in 𝓟; followed by 1837 and all subsequent editions

For gathering 22 of the 1830 edition (pages 337–352, covering Alma 41:8–46:30), page proofing was done against the original manuscript. Thus Oliver Cowdery's mistake in copying *commander* as *captain* into the printer's manuscript was corrected. However, the 1837 edition restored the reading of the printer's manuscript. Both "chief commander" and "chief captain" are found elsewhere in the text. Usually Moroni is referred to as "chief captain" (4 times), but in one place he is referred to as the "chief commander of the armies of the Nephites" (Alma 46:11), nearly the same language as originally in Alma 43:17.

The Existence of Single Readings

Since variation does occur in the text, the correct reading may very well be unique—that is, a particular phrase or word may occur only once in the entire Book of Mormon. Statistically, of course, we expect such cases of singularity, and we should not therefore be overzealous about eliminating exceptional readings.

■ *The Nephites only sought to defend their lives.*

> Alma 54:13   ye have sought to murder us
>   and we have only sought to defend **our lives**
>
> *our lives:* reading in ℗, in Oliver Cowdery's hand
>
> *ourselves:* Oliver Cowdery's misreading, in ℗; followed by 1830 and all subsequent editions

Here the original manuscript reads *our lives.* This usage is unique in the text, so it is not surprising that Oliver Cowdery miscopied the phrase as *ourselves.* The use of "we have only sought to defend our lives" makes a clear contrast with the preceding "ye have sought to murder us" and therefore seems more appropriate than the more prosaic expression "we have only sought to defend ourselves." (The phrase "to defend one's self" occurs 12 times in the text.)

Conjectural Emendation

In studying the Book of Mormon text, we come across cases of possible emendation for which there is no direct manuscript evidence. Nonetheless, it is important to set restrictions on such conjectural emendations. The first requirement for an acceptable conjectural emendation is that there be something inappropriate about the earliest extant readings of the passage (whether printed or in the manuscripts). Evidence regarding the unacceptability of a reading is sometimes referred to as internal evidence since it is based on a conceptual analysis of the language usage within the text. Of course, it may be rather easy to discover something wrong with a particular reading, so we add a second requirement to the first one—namely, there must be some evidence to suggest why the transmitter of the text (whether scribe or typesetter) might have made the error that is presupposed by the conjectural emendation. This second requirement means that we must analyze the errors that the scribes and typesetters typically made as they transmitted the text. This kind of evidence is sometimes referred to as external evidence in that it physically exists in real manuscripts and in actual copies of books. Both these requirements (of internal and external evidence) are necessary in order to prevent conjectural emendation from being excessively applied.

■ *Ishmael and also his whole household were persuaded to leave Jerusalem.*

    1 Nephi 7:5   the Lord did soften the heart of Ishmael
                          and also his **whole household**

        hole hole: scribe 3 in ℗ originally wrote *hole*, then inserted a second *hole* above the line

        household: Oliver Cowdery's interpretation of *hole hole* as *household*, in ℗; followed by
            1830 and all subsequent editions

        whole household: emendation

All other Book of Mormon uses of *household* (11 times) include the universal quantifier (*all, whole,* or the equivalent of *none* in negative contexts). The use of "his hole hole" in the original manuscript suggests that the original text had the phrase "his whole household," which is also found in Alma 22:23 ("his whole household were converted unto the Lord"). When Joseph Smith read off the text for 1 Nephi 7:5, the final *d* of *household* may have been left unpronounced, so that scribe 3 ended up writing down "hole hole," but without the word *house*. (The first *hole* is, of course, a homophone for *whole*.) When copying into the printer's manuscript, Oliver Cowdery emended the impossible reading to "his household"—but without any universal quantifier.

■ *The Bible originally contained the fullness of the gospel of the Lamb, not the gospel of the Land or the gospel of the Lord.*

    1 Nephi 13:24   and when it proceeded forth from the mouth of a Jew
                         it contained the fullness of **the gospel of the Lamb**

        the gospel of the Land: dubious reading in ℗, in scribe 2's hand

        the gospel of the Lord: Oliver Cowdery's interpretation, in ℗; followed by 1830 and
            all subsequent editions

        the gospel of the Lamb: emendation

Scribe 2 of the original manuscript apparently misheard Joseph Smith's *lamb* as *land,* especially since the final *d* of *land* is often silent. When copying into the printer's manuscript, Oliver Cowdery interpreted *Land* as an error for *Lord.* Elsewhere the text only refers to "the gospel of the Lamb" (4 times, all in this same chapter), never "the gospel of the Lord." (This emendation was first proposed by three of my students, Zane Kerby, Merilee Knoll, and Rebecca S. Wilson.)

■ *The gentiles shall not always remain in a state of awful wickedness, not woundedness or blindness.*

    1 Nephi 13:32   neither will the Lord God suffer that
                         the gentiles shall forever remain
                         in that state of awful **wickedness**
                            which thou beholdest that they are in

        woundedneſs: reading in ℗, in scribe 2's hand; copied as such into ℗ by Oliver Cowdery;
            1830 also follows this reading

        blindneſs: Joseph Smith's emendation, in ℗; followed by 1837 and all subsequent editions

        wickedness: emendation

Scribe 2 of the original manuscript wrote down *woundedness,* which is visually similar to *wickedness* (both begin with *w* and end with *edness*). But since the error is probably not an auditory one, it is quite possible that Joseph Smith himself misread the word to his scribe (instead of the scribe mishearing it). Elsewhere the Book of Mormon never refers to a "state of woundedness" (in fact, there are no other examples of the word *woundedness* in the text). On the other hand, there are references to a "state of wickedness" (4 times), and in each case the word *awful* occurs with the expression:

Helaman 4:25	for they had fallen into *a state of unbelief and awful wickedness*
Helaman 7:4	and seeing the people in *a state of such awful wickedness* . . .
3 Nephi 6:17	and thus in the commencement of this the thirtieth year they were in *a state of awful wickedness*
Ether 4:15	behold when ye shall rend that veil of unbelief which doth cause you to remain in *your awful state of wickedness* . . .

Finally, we should note that here in 1 Nephi 13:32 the pronoun *that* ("in that state of awful . . .") refers the reader back to an already mentioned state of the gentiles—namely:

1 Nephi 13:29	and because of these things which are taken away out of the gospel of the Lamb an exceeding great many do stumble yea insomuch that Satan hath great power over them

The last line in verse 29 describes a state of wickedness. Although a metaphorical meaning of spiritual woundedness could be assigned in 1 Nephi 13:32, the word *woundedness* did not seem right to Joseph Smith when he did his editing for the 1837 edition. Thus he emended the word to *blindness.*

■ *The Lord told Nephi that he would shake, not shock, Laman and Lemuel.*

1 Nephi 17:53	stretch forth thine hand again unto thy brethren and they shall not wither before thee but I will **shake** them saith the Lord

> ***shock:*** reading in 𝒪, in Oliver Cowdery's hand; followed by 𝒫, 1830, and all subsequent editions
>
> ***shake:*** emendation

The two following verses (1 Nephi 17:54–55) use the word *shake* to refer to what Nephi did to his rebellious brothers ("the Lord did shake them even according to the word which he had spoken" and "it is the power of the Lord that hath shaken us"). Note, in particular, the added explanation in verse 54: "even according to the word which he had spoken." Other Book of Mormon usage supports *shake,* as in 1 Nephi 2:14 ("my father did speak unto them in the valley of Lemuel with power / being filled with the spirit until their frames did shake before him"). In fact, the word *shock* occurs nowhere else in the Book of Mormon. Oliver Cowdery, the scribe here for 1 Nephi 17:53 of the original manuscript, probably misheard Joseph Smith's *shake* as *shock.*

■ *Happiness is opposed to misery.*

2 Nephi 2:11	righteousness could not be brought to pass neither wickedness **neither happiness nor misery** neither good nor bad

> ***neither holiness nor misery:*** reading in 𝒫, in Oliver Cowdery's hand; 𝒪 not extant; reading followed by 1830 and all subsequent editions
>
> ***neither happiness nor misery:*** emendation

The original manuscript is not extant here, but it probably read *happiness* rather than the visually similar *holiness*. Elsewhere in the text, *misery* is consistently contrasted with *happiness* (9 times). For instance, later on in this same verse, the text again lays out a list of oppositions:

> 2 Nephi 2:11   wherefore if it should be one body
> it must needs remain as dead
> having no life neither death
> nor corruption nor incorruption
> *happiness nor misery*
> neither sense nor insensibility

(This emendation replacing *holiness* with *happiness* was first suggested by Corbin T. Volluz.)

■ *Abinadi will suffer even unto death, not until death.*

> Mosiah 17:10   yea and I will suffer even **unto death**

> ***until death:*** reading in 𝒫, in Oliver Cowdery's hand; 𝒪 not extant; reading followed by 1830 and all subsequent editions

> ***unto death:*** emendation

The original manuscript is not extant here. Oliver Cowdery probably miscopied *unto* as *until* (which is visually similar). Elsewhere, whenever someone's death is described, we get only "unto death" (6 times), never "until death." For instance, later in verse 13, the text refers to Abinadi's death by means of the phrase "yea even unto death." Later, king Noah's death, also by fire, is referred to in the same way:

> Mosiah 19:20   and they were angry with the king
> and caused that he should suffer
> even *unto death* by fire

In Mosiah 17:10, the problematic phrase "suffer even until death" would mean that Abinadi's suffering will extend from that time until the moment of death, which is not what Abinadi intended to say. Rather he was prophesying that he would suffer death for his testimony.

■ *Abinadi's skin was scorched by the burning fagots.*

> Mosiah 17:13   and it came to pass that they took him and bound him
> and **scorched** his skin with fagots yea even unto death

> ***scourged:*** reading in 𝒫, in Oliver Cowdery's hand; 𝒪 not extant; reading followed by 1830 and all subsequent editions

> ***scorched:*** emendation

The original manuscript is not extant here, but Oliver Cowdery probably miscopied the original *scorched* with the visually similar *scourged*. The verb *scourge* "to whip" does not make sense here, especially with fagots (bundles of sticks for burning). The word *scorch* here means "to burn the surface of," in distinction to totally burning up or consuming by fire (a distinction which can be inferred from the definitions in the Oxford English Dictionary). The correct verb *scorch* is used in the following verse:

> Mosiah 17:14   and now when the flames began to *scorch* him
> he cried unto them saying . . .

■ *The city of Mulek was in the land of the Nephites.*

Alma 53:6   Moroni had thus gained a victory
over one of the greatest of the armies of the Lamanites
and had obtained possession of the city Mulek
which was one of the strongest holds of the Lamanites
in **the land of the Nephites**

the land of Nephi: reading in Ⓞ, in Oliver Cowdery's hand; followed by Ⓟ, 1830, and all subsequent editions

the land of the Nephites: emendation

The city of Mulek was in Nephite territory. The land of Nephi was originally settled by Nephi, but was later abandoned to the Lamanites. Elsewhere the Book of Mormon text always uses the phrase "the land of Nephi" to refer to this Lamanite territory (55 times). But in this passage, the text refers to Nephite cities that the Lamanites had captured. There is scribal evidence in the manuscripts that Oliver Cowdery sometimes mixed up his writing of "the people of Nephi" with the "the people of the Nephites," so that the mixup of "the land of Nephi" with "the land of the Nephites" is quite plausible. (This emendation was first suggested by Dale Caswell.)

■ *Shiz slew both men women and children.*

Ether 14:17   and it came to pass that Shiz pursued after Coriantumr
and he did overthrow many cities
and he did slay **both men women and children**
and he did burn the cities thereof

both women and children: reading in Ⓟ, in Oliver Cowdery's hand; Ⓞ not extant; reading followed by 1830 and all subsequent editions

both men women and children: emendation

Usage elsewhere in the text consistently favors the expression "both men women and children":

2 Nephi 9:21   for behold he suffereth the pains of all men
yea the pains of every living creature
both men women and children

Helaman 1:27   . . . slaying the people with a great slaughter
both men women and children

Ether 14:22   but they did march forth
from the shedding of blood to the shedding of blood
leaving the bodies of
both men women and children
strewed upon the face of the land

Ether 15:15   when they were all gathered together
—everyone to the army which he would—
with their wives and their children
both men women and children being armed
with weapons of war . . .

On the other hand, there are no other examples in the original text of "both women and children." (The only example in the current text—in Mormon 4:14—originally read "of women and of children.")

The 1837 edition changed this conjunctive phrase to "both women and children," thus creating a unique but problematic reading.) The original manuscript is not extant for Ether 14:17, but probably included *men*. The eye of the scribe (Oliver Cowdery) may have simply skipped over the word *men* to the -*men* at the end of the next word, *women*.

Numbering People

We now consider a number of textual changes involving the numbering of people, including one conjectural emendation.

■ *The Lamanites will be numbered among the house of Israel.*

> 1 Nephi 15:16   behold I say unto you yea /
> they shall be **numbered** again among the house of Israel

> *numbered:* reading in 𝒪, in scribe 2's hand

> *remembered:* Oliver Cowdery's misreading, in 𝒫; followed by 1830 and all subsequent editions

Scribe 2 of the original manuscript wrote *numbered,* but Oliver Cowdery accidentally copied it as *remembered.* The words are visually similar. As we shall see, usage elsewhere in the Book of Mormon clearly favors *numbered* in this context.

■ *The people of Ammon were numbered among the Nephites.*

> Alma 27:27   and they were **numbered** among the people of Nephi
> and also numbered among the people which were of the church of God

> *they were **numbered** among the people of Nephi:* apparent reading in 𝒪, in Oliver Cowdery's hand; only the last part of the word is extant (namely, *ered*)

> *they were among the people of Nephi:* Oliver Cowdery's misreading, in 𝒫; followed by 1830 and all subsequent editions

Oliver Cowdery accidentally dropped out *numbered* when he copied the text into the printer's manuscript. (The last part of the word is extant in the original manuscript.) The people of Ammon were not actually distributed among the people of Nephi, but lived apart (in the land of Jershon). But they were counted as Nephites (not Lamanites) and also as members of the church. It should also be noted that the use of the phrase "also numbered" in the second clause does not make much sense unless the word *numbered* occurs in the first clause.

■ *Nonbelievers were no longer numbered among the people of God.*

> Alma 1:24   and their names were blotted out
> that they were **numbered** no more among the people of God

> *remembered:* reading in 𝒫, in scribe 2's hand; 𝒪 not extant; reading followed by 1830 and all subsequent editions

> *numbered:* emendation

The original manuscript is no longer extant here. Consistent with all other Book of Mormon usage (38 examples, counting the two changes listed just above), the verb should be *numbered.* As we have just seen (in 1 Nephi 15:16), there is specific scribal evidence for misreading *numbered* as *remembered*. Furthermore, the word *remembered* does not make sense here in Alma 1:24; even though peoples' names may be blotted out, the people themselves are remembered. Moreover, all other passages connect church membership with numbering and not remembering:

Mosiah 26:36	and them that would not confess their sins
	    and repent of their iniquity
	the same were not *numbered*
	    among the people of the church
	and their names were blotted out

Alma 5:57	and behold their names shall be blotted out that the names of the wicked shall not be *numbered* among the names of the righteous
Alma 6:3	the same were rejected and their names were blotted out that their names were not *numbered* among those of the righteous
Moroni 6:7	and if they repented not and confessed not their names were blotted out and they were not *numbered* among the people of Christ

This last conjectural emendation thus makes the entire Book of Mormon systematic in its use of numbering people rather than remembering them.

Yea as an Indicator of Further Explication

There are hundreds of examples of the connective adverb *yea* in the Book of Mormon text. Interestingly, virtually every example represents an attempt to modify, amplify, or explain the meaning of the previous clause. Yet, in a few cases, the connective *yea* seems to be used incorrectly. It turns out that these cases involve errors. In fact, in two cases the *yea* should actually be the word *year*.

■ *In the latter end of the nineteenth year . . .*

Alma 48:21	in the latter end of the nineteenth **year** —notwithstanding their peace amongst themselves— they were compelled reluctantly to contend with their brethren

*the nineteenth **year** / notwithstanding:* reading in Ⓞ, in Oliver Cowdery's hand

*the nineteenth / **yea** notwithstanding:* Oliver Cowdery's scribal error, in Ⓟ; followed by 1830 and other early editions, plus all RLDS editions

*the nineteenth **year** / **yea** notwithstanding:* Orson Pratt's emendation, in 1849; followed by all subsequent LDS editions

In both manuscripts Oliver Cowdery frequently dropped off the final *r* when he wrote the word *year*. In his editing for the 1849 edition, Orson Pratt realized the need for the word *year* in this passage, but he did not recognize that the *yea* was an error for *year*. The purpose of the connective *yea* in the Book of Mormon is to comment or expand on a just-mentioned clause. In Alma 48:21 the *yea* does not serve that function.

■ *And it came to pass in the forty and sixth year . . .*

Helaman 3:3   and it came to pass in the forty and sixth **year** /
                   there were much contentions and many dissensions

    *the forty and sixth / **yea** there were:* reading in ⊙, in Oliver Cowdery's hand; copied as
    such by Oliver Cowdery into ℗; followed by 1830 and all subsequent editions

    *the forty and sixth **year** / there were:* emendation

The original manuscript has only *yea*, but we have many examples of Oliver Cowdery dropping the final *r* of *year* (as in the previous example from Alma 48:21). This passage definitely needs the word *year*, while the use of *yea* here does not provide any comment or expansion on the previous clause.

Eliminating Dittographies

When copying from the original manuscript into the printer's manuscript, the scribe would frequently repeat a portion of the text, usually a small phrase. Such dittographies (or repetitions) were usually caught by the scribe himself or by the 1830 typesetter. For instance, when Oliver Cowdery copied 1 Nephi 1:17 into the printer's manuscript, he first wrote "wherefore after that I have abridged the record of my father of my father." In this instance the dittography is blatantly obvious and Oliver crossed out the repeated "of my father." In this section I propose one example of a possible dittography. In this case the original manuscript is not extant, so we have a case of conjecture. This dittography has also been difficult to notice since it begins with the conjunction *and*. Yet the repeated portion is completely unnecessary and is in fact distracting.

■ *They will be grasped with death and hell and the devil.*

2 Nephi 28:23   yea they are grasped **with death and hell and the devil** /
                   and all that have been seized therewith must stand
                       before the throne of God
                   and be judged according to their works

    *with death and hell / **and death and hell** and the devil:* reading in ℗; ⊙ not extant;
    reading followed by 1830 and all subsequent editions

    with death and hell and the devil: emendation

Elsewhere the Book of Mormon text has nine examples of the phrase "death and hell," and in each instance there is no repetition. Here are two of these examples, both in 2 Nephi, which conjoin the phrase "death and hell" with "the devil":

2 Nephi 9:19   for he delivereth his saints
                   from that awful monster
                   the devil and death and hell
                   and that lake of fire and brimstone
                   which is endless torment

2 Nephi 9:26   they are delivered from that awful monster
death and hell and the devil
and the lake of fire and brimstone
which is endless torment

These last two examples also argue that the clausal break for 2 Nephi 28:23 should come at the end of the complete prepositional phrase "with death and hell and the devil." (This dittography in 2 Nephi 28:23 was first suggested by Nathaniel Skousen.)

Emendation Supported by Chiasmus

Sometimes a conjecture is further supported by the poetic structures found in the Book of Mormon. Here is an example that chiasmus supports.

■ *God is perfectly just and merciful.*

Alma 42:15   . . . that God might be **a perfectly just God** and a merciful God also

     a perfect just God: reading in 𝓟, in Oliver Cowdery's hand; 𝓞 not extant; reading followed by 1830 and all subsequent editions

     a perfectly just God: emendation

In the original manuscript, the lacuna (or gap) for this passage has room for a couple more letters, which suggests the emendation *perfectly*. Another possible emendation is "a perfect and just God" (that is, there was an ampersand between *perfect* and *just*). The overall passage refers to the justice and mercy of God, but not God's perfection. Moreover, the chiastic structure of the larger passage supports the emendation "perfectly just":

A   to bring about the plan of *mercy*
B   to appease the demands of *justice*
B   that God might be a perfectly *just* God
A   and a *merciful* God also

Revising the Text

In certain instances of emendation, we need to distinguish between revision and restoring the original text. In cases of revision, we recognize that the suggested change is probably not what the original text read, but seems necessary for modern readers of the text. One way to avoid such emendations is, of course, to place the revision in a footnote, thus providing an explanation of what the original text either meant or should read. In the following I discuss several possible revisions to the text.

Archaic Word Meanings

Sometimes the word used in the original text has an archaic meaning. It may be quite difficult to understand such archaic uses of a word. In the following example, the scribe apparently replaced such an archaic word by one that seemed, at the moment, more reasonable.

■ *After they had ended the sermon . . .*

Mosiah 19:24   and it came to pass that after they had ended **the sermon**
                  that they returned to the land of Nephi

> *the ceremony:* reading in 𝒫, in Oliver Cowdery's hand (spelled as *cerimony*);
>   𝒪 not extant; reading followed by 1830 and all subsequent editions
>
> *the sermon:* emendation
>
> *speaking:* possible revision

The word *ceremony* does not make sense here, nor is there any older meaning of the word that might work. Earlier in the English language the word *sermon* had the more general meaning "talk or discourse" rather than the more specific modern meaning of "preacher's discourse." The original manuscript is not extant here, but if the scribe for that manuscript had misspelled the word *sermon* as *cermon*, then the word could have been very easily misread as *ceremony*. Since *sermon* seems odd here, just as *ceremony* does, we might consider revising the text by selecting a word more appropriate to the style of the Book of Mormon. However, none of the synonymous words that I can think of (for instance, *discussion* and *conversation*) ever occur in the Book of Mormon. Moreover, nouns like *speech, talk,* and *discourse* have historically changed so that now they often refer to a specific verbal presentation by one person. One possible revision for *sermon* could be to use a nominalized verbal such as *speaking* ("after they had ended speaking"), especially since there are nominalized uses of *speaking* elsewhere in the Book of Mormon. Another possibility would be to use *sermon,* but to explain its earlier meaning in a footnote. (Renee Bangerter first came up with this emendation.)

Unacceptable Hebraisms

The original text of the Book of Mormon has a number of Hebraistic expressions that are difficult to understand. These non-English expressions have generally been edited out of the text. In some cases, alternative revisions are possible, as in the following example.

■ *Lehi knows that Jerusalem must be destroyed.*

1 Nephi 3:16–18   and all this he hath done because of the commandment
                     for he **knoweth** that Jerusalem must be destroyed
                        because of the wickedness of the people
                     for behold they have rejected the words of the prophets

> *knowing:* reading in 𝒪; followed by 𝒫, 1830, and other early editions, plus recent
>   RLDS editions
>
> *knew:* emendation, probably by Joseph Smith, in 1840; followed by later LDS editions
>
> *knoweth* or *knows:* possible revision

The Hebraistic use of the participial form *knowing* could be interpreted in either the present or the past tense—literally, as either "he is knowing" or "he was knowing." English, of course, does not use the stative verb *know* in the progressive. For the 1840 edition, Joseph Smith edited the participial *knowing* to the simple past tense *knew.* However, at the time Nephi spoke these words to his brothers, the city of Jerusalem had not yet been destroyed. The surrounding use of the present tense in this passage suggests therefore that the grammatical revision should have been to the simple present tense, as either *knoweth* or *knows* rather than *knew*. Usage elsewhere in the Book of Mormon favors *knoweth* over *knows*.

Correcting a Primitive Error

Sometimes there are errors which may have occurred on the original plates.

■ *The Lamanites preached the gospel to the less wicked, not the more wicked, of the Gaddianton robbers.*

Helaman 6:37   the Lamanites did hunt the band of robbers of Gaddianton
and they did preach the word of God
among **the less wicked part** of them
insomuch that this band of robbers was utterly destroyed
    from among the Lamanites

    the more wicked part: reading in 𝓟, in Oliver Cowdery's hand; 𝓞 not extant;
      reading followed by 1830 and all subsequent editions

    the less wicked part: possible revision

It is difficult to know when the error entered into the text here. It is possible that it might have actually occurred in Mormon's original record (that is, on the plates). It is clear that Mormon intended to say that the Lamanites eliminated the band of Gaddianton robbers (1) by hunting down the more wicked part of them and (2) by preaching to the less wicked part. It is unreasonable to think that the opposite was the case. The resulting confusion in the text seems to be a conflation of these two opposing ideas.

Supplying an Ellipsis

Occasionally the text has a passage where there is considerable ellipsis (or skipping of a phrase). Some of these ellipses may have occurred in the original plates.

■ *Leaders of churches and teachers shall be lifted up in the pride of their hearts.*

Mormon 8:28   yea it shall come in a day
when the power of God shall be denied
and churches become defiled
and shall be lifted up in the pride of their hearts
yea even in a day when leaders of churches and teachers
    shall be lifted up in the pride of their hearts

    leaders of churches and teachers in the pride of their hearts: reading in both 𝓟 and 1830;
      followed by subsequent editions except for recent LDS ones

    *leaders of churches and teachers **shall rise** in the pride of their hearts:* third printing of
      1905 LDS edition; followed by all subsequent LDS editions

    *leaders of churches and teachers **shall be lifted up** in the pride of their hearts:* possible
      revision

Here both the printer's manuscript and the 1830 edition were copied from the original manuscript. Both are missing a finite verb phrase before the second "in the pride of their hearts," which means that the original manuscript probably read the same. It is possible that the original text actually read this way—that is, the text here may represent a case of intended ellipsis. For his 1907 revision of the 1905 Chicago missionary edition, German Ellsworth revised the text by supplying "shall rise" as the ellipted finite verb phrase. However, a more plausible revision would be "shall be lifted up," based on the preceding "and churches become defiled and shall be lifted up in the pride of their hearts."

Conclusions

Ultimately we must realize that the original English-language text of the Book of Mormon is not fully recoverable by human effort. Textual errors are generally not found except by discovering the correct reading in the manuscripts. Unfortunately, only 28 percent of the original manuscript is extant. Conjecture based on internal analysis of the Book of Mormon text has largely been unsuccessful in recovering the correct reading. Still, some conjectures are probably correct. Another important point to keep in mind is that even if we had the entire original manuscript, there would still be errors in the text, mainly because the original manuscript itself has some errors.

The systematic nature of the original text supports the theory that the text was revealed to Joseph Smith word for word. On the other hand, all subsequent transmissions of the text appear to have been subject to human error. Errors have crept into the text, but no error significantly interferes with either the message of the book or its doctrine. These textual errors have never prevented readers of the book from receiving their own personal witness of its truth. ▰

A Response: "What the Manuscripts and the Eyewitnesses Tell Us about the Translation of the Book of Mormon"

DANIEL C. PETERSON

ROYAL SKOUSEN has devoted a decade and a half to intensive study of the text of the Book of Mormon, and most especially to the original and printer's manuscripts of the book.[1] It is his strongly considered opinion that the manuscript evidence supports the traditional account of the origin of the Book of Mormon, and that it doesn't support the notion that Joseph Smith composed the text himself or took it from any other existing manuscript. Yet all the witnesses thought that Joseph Smith somehow saw words and read them off to his scribes.[2] Taken together, these two facts are highly significant. Let us briefly examine some of the relevant data.

First of all, the evidence strongly supports the traditional account in saying that the original manuscript was orally dictated. The kinds of errors that occur in the manuscript are clearly those that occur from a scribe mishearing, rather than from visually misreading while copying from another manuscript. (The printer's manuscript, by contrast, shows precisely the types of anomalies that one would expect from a copyist's errors.) Royal's meticulous analysis even suggests that Joseph was working with up to twenty to thirty words at a time.[3]

It is apparent that Joseph could see the spelling of names on whatever it was that he was reading from.[4]

When the scribe had written the text, he (or she in the case of Emma Smith) would evidently read it back to Joseph Smith for correction.[5] So the Prophet evidently had something with him from which he was dictating, and against which he could check what his scribes had written. But what was it? The witnesses are unanimous that he did not have any books or manuscripts or papers with him during the translation process, which involved lengthy periods of dictation.[6]

In an interview with her son, Joseph Smith III, not long before she died, Emma Smith insisted that Joseph had no text with him during the work of translation:

> Q. Had he not a book or manuscript from which he read, or dictated to you?
>
> A. He had neither manuscript nor book to read from.
>
> Q. Could he not have had, and you not know it?
>
> A. If he had had anything of the kind he could not have concealed it from me.

Emma Smith could speak authoritatively regarding the period during which she herself served as scribe. But what about the much longer period when Oliver Cowdery was taking the dictation? In fact, Emma could speak from personal experience with respect to that time, as well. While they were in Harmony, Pennsylvania—where most of the Book of Mormon text was committed to writing—Emma says that Joseph and Oliver were not far away from her:

Q. Where did father and Oliver Cowdery write?
A. Oliver Cowdery and your father wrote in the room where I was at work.

"The plates," she said, "often lay on the table without any attempt at concealment, wrapped in a small linen table cloth, which I had given him to fold them in. I once felt of the plates as they thus lay on the table, tracing their outline and shape. They seemed to be pliable like thick paper, and would rustle with a metallic sound when the edges were moved by the thumb, as one does sometimes thumb the edges of a book."[7]

Not long after speaking with her, Joseph III wrote a letter in which he summarized some of her responses to his questions. "She wrote for Joseph Smith during the work of translation, as did also Reuben Hale, her brother, and O. Cowdery; that the larger part of this labor was done in her presence, and where she could see and know what was being done; that during no part of it did Joseph Smith have any mss. [manuscripts] or book of any kind from which to read, or dictate, except the metallic plates, which she knew he had."[8]

A correspondent from the *Chicago Times* interviewed David Whitmer on 14 October 1881, and got the same story: "Mr. Whitmer emphatically asserts as did Harris and Cowdery, that while Smith was dictating the translation he had no manuscript notes or other means of knowledge save the seer stone and the characters as shown on the plates, he [i.e., David Whitmer] being present and cognizant how it was done."[9]

Similarly, the *St. Louis Republican*, based upon an interview in mid-July of 1884, reported that "Father Whitmer, who was present very frequently during the writing of this manuscript [i.e., of the Book of Mormon] affirms that Joseph Smith had no book or manuscript, before him from which he could have read as is asserted by some that he did, he (Whitmer) having every opportunity to know whether Smith had Solomon Spaulding's or any other person's romance [i.e., a novel] to read from."[10]

David Whitmer repeatedly insisted that the translation process occurred in full view of Joseph

Smith's family and associates. (The common image of a curtain hanging between the Prophet and his scribes, sometimes seen in illustrations of the story of the Book of Mormon, is based on a misunderstanding. There was indeed a curtain, at least in the latter stages of the translation process. However, that curtain was suspended not between the translator and his scribe but near the front door of the Peter Whitmer home, in order to prevent idle passersby and gawkers from interfering with the work.[11])

Further evidence that, whatever else was happening, Joseph Smith was not simply reading from a manuscript, comes from an episode recounted by David Whitmer to William H. Kelley and G. A. Blakeslee in January 1882:

He could not translate unless he was humble and possessed the right feelings towards every one. To illustrate, so you can see. One morning when he was getting ready to continue the translation, something went wrong about the house and he was put out about it. Something that Emma, his wife, had done. Oliver and I went up stairs, and Joseph came up soon after to continue the translation, but he could not do anything. He could not translate a single syllable. He went down stairs, out into the orchard and made supplication to the Lord; was gone about an hour—came back to the house, asked Emma's forgiveness and then came up stairs where we were and the translation went on all right. He could do nothing save he was humble and faithful.[12]

Whitmer told the same story to a correspondent for the *Omaha Herald* during an interview on 10 October 1886. In perhaps somewhat overwrought language, the Herald's reporter summarized the account as follows:

He [Joseph Smith] went into the woods again to pray, and this time was gone fully an hour. His friends became positively concerned, and were about to institute a search, when Joseph entered the room, pale and haggard, having suffered a vigorous chastisement at the hands of the Lord. He went straight in humiliation to his wife, entreated and received her forgiveness, returned to his work, and, much to the joy of himself and his anxious friends surrounding him, the stone again glared forth its letters of fire.[13]

It would seem from this anecdote that Joseph Smith needed to be spiritually or emotionally ready for the translation process to proceed—something that would have been wholly unnecessary if he had simply been reading from a prepared manuscript. At this point, a skeptic might perhaps suggest that emotional distractions interfered with Joseph Smith's ability to remember a text that he had memorized the night before for dictation to his naive secretaries, or that personal upheavals distracted him from improvising an original text for them to write down as it occurred to him. But such potential counter-explanations run into their own very serious difficulties: Whether it is even remotely plausible to imagine Joseph Smith or anyone else memorizing or composing nearly 5000 words daily, day after day, week after week, in the production of a lengthy and complex book is a question that readers can ponder for themselves. One might also ask the same skeptic why Joseph would not just have written out the text himself if he were indeed faking reception of the text by revelation.

An anecdote recounted by Martin Harris to Edward Stevenson seems to argue against the translation process being either the simple dictation of a memorized text or the mechanical reading of an ordinary manuscript surreptitiously smuggled into the room. Harris is speaking about the earliest days of the work, before the arrival of Oliver Cowdery, when he was serving as scribe. Harris "said that the Prophet possessed a seer stone, by which he was enabled to translate as well as from the Urim and Thummim, and for convenience he then used the seer stone."[14] The seer stone was placed in a hat in order to obscure the surrounding light and make the deliverances from the stone easier to see. By contrast, of course, the scribes needed light in order to be able to write down the text. This situation, coupled with the lack of a dividing curtain, would have made it very difficult, if not impossible, for Joseph to have concealed a manuscript, or books, or the plates themselves. Stevenson's account continues:

> By aid of the seer stone, sentences would appear and were read by the Prophet and written by Martin, and when finished he would say, "Written," and if correctly written, that sentence would disappear and another appear in its place, but if not written correctly it remained until corrected, so that the translation was just as it was engraven on the plates, precisely in the language then used. Martin said, after continued translation they would become weary, and would go

down to the river and exercise by throwing stones out on the river, etc. While so doing on one occasion, Martin found a stone very much resembling the one used for translating, and on resuming their labor of translation, Martin put in place the stone that he had found. He said that the Prophet remained silent, unusually and intently gazing in darkness, no traces of the usual sentences appearing. Much surprised, Joseph exclaimed, "Martin! What is the matter? All is as dark as Egypt!" Martin's countenance betrayed him, and the Prophet asked Martin why he had done so. Martin said, to stop the mouths of fools, who had told him that the Prophet had learned those sentences and was merely repeating them, etc.[15]

Furthermore, it is clear from careful analysis of the original manuscript that Joseph did not know in advance what the text was going to say. Chapter breaks and book divisions apparently surprised him. He would see some indication, evidently, of a break in the text, and, in each case, would tell his scribe to write "Chapter." The numbers were then added later. For instance, at what we now recognize as the end of 1 Nephi, the original manuscript first indicates merely that a new chapter is about to begin. (In the original chapter divisions, that upcoming text was marked as "Chapter VIII.") When Joseph and Oliver subsequently discovered that they were instead at the opening of a wholly distinct book, 2 Nephi, the original chapter specification was crossed out and placed after the title of the new book. This is quite instructive. It indicates that Joseph could only see the end of a section but did not know whether the next section would be another portion of the same book or, rather, the commencement of an entirely new book.[16]

Moreover, there were parts of the text that he did not understand. "When he came to proper names he could not pronounce, or long words," his wife Emma recalled of the earliest part of the translation, "he spelled them out."[17] And she evidently mentioned her experience to David Whitmer or else he knew of this phenomenon by other, independent, means. "When Joseph could not pronounce the words," Whitmer told E. C. Briggs and Rudolph Etzenhouser in 1884, "he spelled them out letter by letter."[18] Briggs also recalled an 1856 interview with Emma Smith in which "she remarked of her husband Joseph's limited education while he was translating the Book of Mormon, and she was scribe at the time, 'He could not pronounce the word Sariah.' And one time while translating, where it speaks of the walls of Jerusalem, he stopped and said, 'Emma, did Jerusalem have walls surrounding it?' When I informed him it had, he replied, 'O, I thought I was deceived.'"[19] As the *Chicago Tribune* summarized David Whitmer's testimony in 1885, he confirmed Emma's experience: "In translating the characters Smith, who was *illiterate and but little* versed in Biblical lore, was ofttimes compelled to spell the words out, not knowing the correct pronunciation, and Mr. Whitmer recalls the fact that at that time Smith did not even know that Jerusalem was a walled city."[20] (The use of the term *illiterate* is potentially misleading here since Joseph Smith was literate, given the now-current meaning of the word. He could read and he could write. But Joseph was not a learned person; he was not a man of letters. Accordingly, in one sense of the word, he was illiterate.[21])

In its notice of the death of David Whitmer, and undoubtedly based upon its prior interviews with him, the 24 January 1888 issue of the *Chicago Times* again alluded to the difficulties Joseph Smith had with the text he was dictating: "Smith being an illiterate, would often stumble over big words, which the village schoolmaster [Oliver Cowdery] would pronounce for him, and so the work proceeded."[22]

Thus we see that Joseph Smith seems to have been reading from something, but that he had no book or manuscript or paper with him. It seems to have been a text that was new and strange to him, and one that required a certain emotional or mental focus before it could be read. All of this is entirely consistent with Joseph Smith's claim that he was deriving the text by revelation through an interpreting device, but it does not seem reconcilable with claims that he had created the text himself earlier, or even that he was reading from a purloined copy of someone else's manuscript. In order to make the latter theory plausible, it is necessary to reject the unanimous testimony of the eyewitnesses to the process and to ignore the evidence of the original manuscript itself. ■

NOTES

1. For the results of his labors thus far, see Royal Skousen, ed., *The Original Manuscript of the Book of Mormon: Typographical Facsimile of the Extant Text* (Provo, Utah: FARMS, 2001); Royal Skousen, ed., *The Printer's Manuscript of the Book of Mormon: Typographical Facsimile of the Entire Text in Two Parts* (Provo, Utah: FARMS, 2001).

2. See Royal Skousen, "Translating the Book of Mormon: Evidence from the Original Manuscript," in *Book of Mormon Authorship Revisited: The Evidence for Ancient Origins,* ed., Noel B. Reynolds (Provo, Utah: FARMS, 1997), 61–93. A revised and shorter version of the same article has been published as Royal Skousen, "How Joseph Smith Translated the Book of Mormon: Evidence from the Original Manuscript," *Journal of Book of Mormon Studies* 7/1 (1998): 22–31. Lyndon W. Cook, *David Whitmer Interviews: A Restoration Witness* (Orem, Utah: Grandin Book Company, 1991), is replete with testimony to this effect.

3. Skousen, "Translating the Book of Mormon," 67–75; Skousen, "How Joseph Smith Translated the Book of Mormon," 25.

4. Skousen, "Translating the Book of Mormon," 75–82; Skousen, "How Joseph Smith Translated the Book of Mormon," 27.

5. Skousen, "Translating the Book of Mormon," 82–84; Skousen, "How Joseph Smith Translated the Book of Mormon," 27.

6. See Skousen, "Translating the Book of Mormon," 62; Skousen, "How Joseph Smith Translated the Book of Mormon," 24.

7. Joseph Smith III, "Last Testimony of Sister Emma," *Saints' Advocate* 2/4 (October 1879): 50–52; *Saints' Herald* 26/19 (1 October 1879): 289–90.

8. Letter of Joseph Smith III to James T. Cobb, dated 14 February 1879, Letterbook 2, pp. 85–88, RLDS Archives. Cited in Richard Lloyd Anderson, *Investigating the Book of Mormon Witnesses* (Salt Lake City: Deseret Book, 1981), 29.

9. *Chicago Times* (17 October 1881), as given in Cook, *David Whitmer Interviews,* 76. Compare Whitmer's reply to J. W. Chatburn, as reported in *Saints' Herald* 29 (15 June 1882), and reproduced in Cook, *David Whitmer Interviews,* 92.

10. *St. Louis Republican* (16 July 1884), as given in Cook, *David Whitmer Interviews,* 139–40.

11. See his comments to the *Chicago Tribune* (17 December 1885), as also the summary of an interview with him given in a February 1870 letter from William E. McLellin to some unidentified "dear friends" and the report published in the *Chicago Times* (24 January 1888). The relevant passages are conveniently available in Cook, *David Whitmer Interviews,* 173, 233–34, 249; for early use of a curtain, see Skousen, "Translating the Book of Mormon," 63–64.

12. Cook, *David Whitmer Interviews,* 86.

13. *Omaha Herald* (17 October 1886), as reprinted in Cook, *David Whitmer Interviews,* 199.

14. Edward Stevenson, "One of the Three Witnesses: Incidents in the Life of Martin Harris," *Millennial Star* 44 (6 February 1882): 86.

15. Stevenson, "One of the Three Witnesses," 86–87.

16. See Skousen, *Original Manuscript,* 164; also Skousen, "Translating the Book of Mormon," 85–86; Skousen, "How Joseph Smith Translated the Book of Mormon," 27–28.

17. Edmund C. Briggs, "A Visit to Nauvoo in 1856," *Journal of History* 9 (January 1916): 454.

18. Said in a 25 April 1884 interview with E. C. Briggs and Rudolph Etzenhouser, published in *Saints' Herald* 31 (21 June 1884), as given in Cook, *David Whitmer Interviews,* 128. By the time Joseph reached the portion of the Book of Mormon translation that is still extant in the original manuscript, there seems to be little if any evidence of such spelling out; see Skousen, "Translating the Book of Mormon," 76–78.

19. Cited in Cook, *David Whitmer Interviews,* 126–27. In a personal communication dated 18 August 2001, Royal Skousen suggests, plausibly enough, that Joseph probably kept pronouncing *Sariah* as *Sarah.*

20. *Chicago Tribune* (17 December 1885), as given in Cook, *David Whitmer Interviews,* 174. Emphasis in the original. Whitmer also mentioned the walls-of-Jerusalem incident in a conversation with M. J. Hubble, on 13 November 1886. See Cook, *David Whitmer Interviews,* 211.

21. The use of *literate* in the sense of *learned* is found in the Oxford English Dictionary, under *literate.* But it is not found under *illiterate;* there we basically have only the meaning of "not able to read or write."

22. *Chicago Times* (24 January 1888), as reproduced in Cook, *David Whitmer Interviews,* 249.